The Transforming Fire
of **Divine Love**

"John Armstrong's pastorally sensitive theological reflection and his vulnerable personal narrative will help to empower and inspire readers as they seek to understand and embody Christian convictions."

—**Gary Chartier**, La Sierra University

"In this book, John Armstrong invites the reader on a journey to discover the wonder of embracing in humble faith that 'God is love.' He helps his audience discern unwarranted limitations of that bold but comforting truth as they have developed in Christian history, opening up about his own development of a greater appreciation for the wisdom of the broader Christian tradition—Catholic, Orthodox, and Protestant. There is much to learn and appreciate here."

—**James R. Payton Jr.**, professor of patristics and historical theology, McMaster Divinity College

"In *The Transforming Fire of Divine Love*, John Armstrong presents us with a morally serious vision of the Christian God, whose love is cleansing and restorative. This book is recommended for all who want to reflect on the God who is love and perhaps even experience its life-changing warmth."

—**Jordan Wessling**, assistant professor of religion, Lindsey Wilson College

"*The Transforming Fire of Divine Love* lifts us above a world blind to the Father's love, to the love that is theological, ecclesiastical, and personal. John Armstrong lives deeply in the truth that 'God is love.' All our 'love words and actions' are measured by this eternal Trinitarian reality. This divine love has been received and passed on by the Spirit-born body of Christ, the church. He has searched far and wide in this holy tradition to journey into the beauty of this love. He has witnessed to his own pilgrimage, through time and struggle, to journey into the personal reality of this wondrous love. His own story is a humble testimony that the divine love is the overflow of eternal love by participating in the suffering of the cross. I am grateful for this book!"

—**Wilbur David Ellsworth**, archpriest, Holy Transfiguration Antiochian Orthodox Church, Warrenville, Illinois

"John's central thesis is that the truth that God is love lies at the heart of all divine revelation. Cliche? Hardly! It lies at the very heart of Scripture and the Orthodox *Divine Liturgy of St John Chrysostom*. Readers will learn of God's love in Scripture, but even more, they will experience God's love in spiritually practical ways. Highly recommended!"

—**Bradley Nassif**, pastor, Holy Transfiguration Antiochian Orthodox Church, Warrenville, Illinois

"Explorers travel to new places. Some travel in their thought life. If some of John's references don't alarm you then, you haven't read him closely. John's intellect requires challenge, depth, and difference. I'm really not worthy to endorse this book, but I can endorse John's life of God-love. It's real."

—**Jim Henderson**, co-author of *Jim and Casper Go to Church*

The Transforming Fire
of **Divine Love**

My Long, Slow Journey into the Love of God

John H. Armstrong

Foreword by Wes Granberg-Michaelson

CASCADE *Books* • Eugene, Oregon

THE TRANSFORMING FIRE OF DIVINE LOVE
My Long, Slow Journey into the Love of God

Copyright © 2025 John H. Armstrong. All rights reserved. Except for brief quotations in critical publications or reviews, no part of this book may be reproduced in any manner without prior written permission from the publisher. Write: Permissions, Wipf and Stock Publishers, 199 W. 8th Ave., Suite 3, Eugene, OR 97401.

Cascade Books
An Imprint of Wipf and Stock Publishers
199 W. 8th Ave., Suite 3
Eugene, OR 97401

www.wipfandstock.com

PAPERBACK ISBN: 979-8-3852-2741-9
HARDCOVER ISBN: 979-8-3852-2742-6
EBOOK ISBN: 979-8-3852-2743-3

Cataloguing-in-Publication data:

Names: Armstrong, John H., author. | Wes Granberg-Michaelson, foreword.

Title: The transforming fire of divine love : my long, slow journey into the love of God / John H. Armstrong; foreword by Wes Granberg-Michaelson.

Description: Eugene, OR: Cascade Books, 2025 | Includes bibliographical references and index.

Identifiers: ISBN 979-8-3852-2741-9 (paperback) | ISBN 979-8-3852-2742-6 (hardcover) | ISBN 979-8-3852-2743-3 (ebook)

Subjects: LCSH: God (Christianity)—Love.

Classification: BT140 A75 2025 (paperback) | BT140 (ebook)

VERSION NUMBER 02/13/25

All Scripture quotations, unless otherwise indicated, are taken from *New Revised Standard Version Updated Edition*, copyright 2021, National Council of Churches of Christ in the United States of America.

For my twin grandsons, Kobe and Kaleb.
You have both made our life together richer by sharing our home.
I love you more than you will ever know and pray you too will
experience the transforming fire of God's love.

Contents

Foreword by Wes Granberg-Michaelson | ix
Preface | xiii
Acknowledgments | xvii

Chapter One
The Fire That Transforms | 1

Chapter Two
An Astonishing Statement | 9

Chapter Three
The Bible Tells Me So | 19

Chapter Four
Creation: The Gift of Love | 28

Chapter Five
Love Is Who God Is | 40

Chapter Six
Can God's Love Be Defined? | 50

Chapter Seven
Does Love Suffer? | 62

Chapter Eight
A Theology of Love | 74

Chapter Nine
Is Love All We Need? | 86

Chapter Ten
Abba: Knowing God Intimately | 97

Chapter Eleven
Love Takes Human Flesh | 108

Chapter Twelve
The Trinity of Love | 122

Chapter Thirteen
Amazing Love: The Death and Resurrection of Christ | 136

Chapter Fourteen
Misconceptions | 151

Chapter Fifteen
Can We Experience God's Love? | 166

Postscript | 179
Bibliography | 181

Foreword

JOHN 3:16 WAS THE first Bible verse I memorized. Most likely it is the single most memorized verse of Scripture. The reference even appears on signs in the end zones of televised football games. It's like the Magna Carta of evangelicalism. But it also may be one of the most misunderstood verses of the Bible.

"God so loved the world that he gave his only Son . . ." is not a prelude to an altar call with a half-sentence of an atonement theology. Rather, it is a profound glimpse into the scope of God's love for the whole "cosmos" (the world), the nature of God's self-giving love, and the relational love of the Trinity. It's just one of a multitude of biblical declarations, metaphors, prayers, and parables testifying that God is love. Said differently, that God's essence and presence is known most fully as God's Love. This is what John Armstrong is explaining, with care and passion, on the following pages of this insightful book, *The Transforming Fire of Divine Love*.

Focusing on God's love—what Armstrong comes to call "God-Love" since this is not an attribute of God, but God's being—is where all theology should begin and find its foundation. But it doesn't. This book sheds some light on how and why. Various theologies miss this central reality by minimizing, qualifying, and diminishing the bedrock truth that God is love. In part, that's because this cannot be apprehended simply through the mind, intellectually. It's known in ways beyond knowing, relationally, and in communion. It comes true amid clouds of unknowing, in images where vines and branches are one, and within indisputable visions of fourteenth-century women in isolated anchor-holds.

All this can be theologically inconvenient. Rational systems attempting to comprehensively explain all the truth about faith seem to falter. Embracing God and Love as one indissoluble identity leaves too many unanswered questions. Theologies that provide rationalizations for perplexing contradictions feel more comfortable. More than that, as Armstrong points out, our ideas about God's nature are often our own projections born from childhood experiences, cultural assumptions, and legal, moralistic systems.

Yet, the theological task is essential. John Armstrong shares the theological and spiritual journey of a lifetime to demonstrate why it is so crucial, and so clearly within our grasp, to retrieve the full, powerful, embracing truth that God is Love. He does so with deep theological grounding supported by convincing biblical insight. This may be the book's most important contribution to the wider church.

Affirming the essential unity, in being and doing, of God and Love illuminates our understanding of who we are as those created in God's image. God's nature has consequences that are directly derivative for human nature. This overturns various theological mindsets. For instance, theologies that begin with an assumption of human wretchedness and God's wrath are facing a long overdue reckoning. Armstrong helps provide this. He writes: "We are beloved persons created for divine love." And that's not where we are supposed to end up. That's where we start.

We need to recover this starting point, desperately, for the sake of Christianity's future within Western culture, and for the sake of this world's future, so loved by God. This book serves as a guide for such a recovery process. And that journey is not circumscribed by the binary categories of conservative vs. liberal theology. The fifteen chapters of this book reveal the trajectory, the obstacles, the discoveries, and the joy of this journey. The book's subtitle, *My Long, Slow Journey into the Love of God*, alerts us to how these pages are not simply a theological exploration, but also a personal recapitulation of John's abiding Christian faith. While not a memoir, the book reveals how the earnest search to grasp God's Love emerges from and is woven into Armstrong's pilgrimage as a follower of Jesus Christ.

John Armstrong has a deeply rooted evangelical faith that has grown branches that reach widely into ecumenical spaces. His broad theological wisdom doesn't hesitate to dissect the restrictive, limiting blinders of his earlier views, and harvests essential gleanings from a broad diversity of theological traditions. He turns our attention to Catholic theological voices that have creatively explored the depth of God's love, and draws from early mystics and contemplatives who have shared not only their knowledge but their participation in this mystery of love.

Wisdom from the Orthodox tradition, so often overlooked or unknown in the evangelical and then Reformed world that provide a home base for Armstrong, are explicated with rich, appreciative inquiry. That becomes crucial for describing what God's nature as Love, outpoured for humanity, means for the possibility of one to participate in this Love, belonging as sons and daughters to God's life. Ancient wisdom from church "fathers" is blended with insights from contemporary Orthodox theologians as new windows into God's nature, and our own, are opened.

The book notes how voices like Desmond Tutu approached grasping God as Love within their fraught contexts, and the place of process theologians and other historic Protestant voices. All this provides a wide ecumenical breadth to the focused exploration of what it means to know that God is Love. This provides an approach that is evangelical but ecumenical, Reformed but always reforming, Catholic but not dogmatic, Orthodox but spiritually inquisitive, and Christocentric but Trinitarian. That theological framework also describes John Armstrong's life and witness. What he writes he lives.

Frederick Buechner has written, "To say that God is love is either the last straw or the ultimate truth." *The Fire of Transforming Love* asks you to make that choice. But in the end, this is not an intellectual decision but a relational invitation. Ilia Delio, the Franciscan theologian and scientist, provides this explanation: "When I speak about love as core reality to colleagues in theology (or science) I often get a look of annoyance or the raised eyebrows that signify dismissal. . . . I want to shout out . . . but often I remain silent because love cannot be defended by analytical arguments: love has its own internal logic. . . . I went in search of truth and found love at the heart of all things."

The first chapter of this book explores the biblical connection between fire and divine love, reflected in the book's title. In addition to the examples Armstrong provides, that draws me to the passage from Malachi 3:2, "He is like a refiner's fire." It's a bass aria in Handel's *Messiah*. But the background is illuminating. In ancient times gold embedded in rocks was crushed, washed, and then subjected to high temperature in furnaces that removed impurities, or the "dross," to reveal its true essence. In this process, the goldsmith would know that its essence has been revealed when the image of his face is reflected back in the emerging gold material.

The protective layers of our dross hide the truth of our essence, held in God's Love, and holding God's image. The refiner's fire liberates us, inviting us into those moments where the gaze of God's Love is reflected back. Then the circuit is complete as Love returns Love. This is the Love that then shines as the liberating Light of the world.

The Transforming Fire of God's Love beckons you to participate in this mystery.

Wes Granberg-Michaelson
Santa Fe, New Mexico
Advent, 2024

Preface

I HAVE LIVED WITH the writing of this book since 2012. Small portions of two chapters appeared as part of my earlier book, *Costly Love: The Way to True Unity for All the Followers of Jesus* (New City Press, 2017). When I wrote *Costly Love* I intended to have the first half of that book be about divine love. But alas, that book would have been far too long so painful cuts were made. The rest of that 269-page book became a call to *live* God's love through faith, hope and love, i.e., what I called *costly love*. I made the case for how the love of God exhorts us to love our neighbors, our family, our friends, even our enemies (Matt 22:36–40; 5:42–44; John 15:13). The underlying theme can be seen in my subtitle.

My personal mission, for the past thirty-five years, has been to teach and live the visible generous unity we have with Jesus and others through the mystery of divine love. This unity was present in the love of Jesus and the Father that existed "before the foundation of the world" (John 17:24; cf. 17:5). In the well-known prayer of John 17 Jesus expressed his intention to *share* this life, the life of love he had with his Father, with all those who would believe in him (e.g., John 17:26). He clearly indicates that this life is a sharing in the divine love experienced by those who are in union with Christ. I believe the point is clear; God has a deep and abiding love for us. For this reason the more I sought to live out my vision of oneness with others the more I wanted to know the love of God, which I came to see in the love of the Trinity: the Father, the Son, and the Holy Spirit. Looking back, I can now see that it was divine love that empowered me to trust God with this calling to seek oneness with others when the skies in my own life became the darkest.

So this book is what might be called a "prequel." If I had a do-over I would have written this book first. But feeling compelled to now write it, all these years later, has allowed me a great deal of time to read large portions of academic and popular writing on divine love. This time has also allowed me to embrace and practice several spiritual disciplines that have brought me into a deeper experience of God's love for me. The more I researched, wrote, and prayed, the more I knew I did not understand this subject as well as I should. (I also realized that no one ever grasps divine love, or any divine truth for that matter, at least as deeply as they would like.) I returned again and again to my questions and pursued a deeper understanding of the primary theological texts that show how the whole church (Catholic–Protestant–Orthodox) has understood the love of God. As a teacher of the Scripture I searched hundreds of biblical texts. I discovered life-changing truth, truth that helped me pray and reflect on this central question: "What does it mean to believe that God is love?" Even more importantly, "Can I experience God's love as a healing stream flowing in and through my inner being?"

My central thesis, therefore, lies in this straightforward conclusion—*the truth that God is love lies at the heart of all divine revelation.* For the Christian, God *is* love gets everything right, thus this affirmation should be the true and unique confession of the whole (catholic) Christian church. (Ironically the earliest creeds do *not* mention divine love directly!)

Over the past eight years I have started this book a number of times but hit one wall after another. One issue I had to continually face was my own physical weakness. For twenty-five years I have dealt with a chronic illness that saps my energy, often in profound ways. On top of this I had COVID in late 2023, which seems to have increased my fatigue and related complications in my compromised immune system. This fatigue syndrome (ME/CFS) impacts my sleep and creates what is called "brain fog." I am profoundly weary most all the time and often have only small windows of strength within which I can do just so much. In every other way I am healthy, for which I give thanks. But this daily tribulation complicates every aspect of my life, especially my reading and writing. Second, I have found this subject to be such a deep ocean of truth that the more I studied and wrote the more I realized I would never reach the bottom. However, in my very weakness divine love became the truth that transformed me like no other I have ever known.

If you undertake a journey to the love of God you too will eventually have to face questions that cannot be simplistically answered. The questions I ask in this book are meant to drive you to God, the One who loves you more than you can possibly know. Make no mistake about this—you must discover for yourself that God is love!

It was precisely here, in sheer silence before God, that I began to encounter divine mystery. There is clearly more to see, and much, much more to experience, but first you must grasp the smallest glimmer of divine love and then plunge into the depths of God's love for you.

Finally, though I generally set my own parameters in writing, I am well aware of just how much content readers can digest in these frenetic times. Various forms of media have turned us into passive receptors more than active contemplatives. Recent brain research suggests that screens have a deleterious impact on our thought process. For a host of reasons careful reading has fast become a lost discipline. To this end I have made some editorial decisions that I hope will assist you. Let me explain.

My target audience is not academics but serious readers who wish to think about God and eternal love. I hope you will ask questions, lots of questions. These questions can lead you step by step into divine love by firing your imagination for what is beyond natural reason. But first you must open your mind and heart to begin this journey into love.

While I employ academic sources from across the Christian tradition—Catholic, Orthodox, and Protestant—I try to avoid technical jargon in my attempt to explain the truth that "God is love." (When I use certain terms I will provide simple definitions in my notes.)

I propose, therefore, to explore what Charles Wesley called the "strange design" of God's love. I believe divine love is indeed "strange," especially today. I believe this is true because love is eternally beautiful yet we live in a time that has too little taste for real beauty. True beauty takes us beyond our natural way of seeing and unsettles us with mystery. If God is love then I submit that nothing could be more worthwhile for the serious God-seeker than to plunge into the ocean of eternal love.

The former Archbishop of Canterbury, Rowan Williams, once said that the mystical visions of Julian of Norwich (written in the late fourteenth century) "may be the most important work of Christian reflection in the English language."[1] I agree.

Julian wrote about her experience of God as love in words that frame her classic book.

---

1. *Julian of Norwich: Selections from* Revelations of Divine Love—*Annotated and Explained,* citation from the back cover.

At the same time, our Lord showed me a spiritual vision of his familiar love. I saw that for us he is everything that we find good and comforting. He is our clothing, wrapping us for love, embracing and enclosing us for tender love, so that he can never leave us, being himself everything that is good for us, as I understand it.[2]

My prayer for you is simple. *May you know and see the love of God.* And may the profound congruence between God, and his divine image in you, be *clearly revealed to your mind and heart* so that the wide range of biblical words and thoughts used here will assist you in knowing, perhaps as never before, that God is love.

---

2. *Julian of Norwich*, 21. Mary Earle suggests that Julian used this image because Norwich was a textile center. The reference to her clothing was a way of saying that God was part of her daily life and as close to her as her clothing.

Acknowledgments

My books have always required the generous investment of friends. This book is no exception. My friends are a true display of what divine love looks like.

I am especially grateful to my publisher for solid support. Rodney Clapp, my editor, became a trusted friend long before he became my editor. His gracious listening and interaction were truly valuable once again.

James Stock, the marketing director at Cascade, has helped me and, in the process, become my friend. His love for the Oregon Ducks matches mine for the Alabama Crimson Tide.

Gregory Morrison, associate professor of library sciences at Wheaton College, goes back with me to my earliest days as a pastor. He has also become a good friend and provided constant help in finding what I needed for research.

I am especially thankful for Rev. Dr. Wesley Granberg-Michaelson, general secretary emeritus of the Reformed Church in America. Wes welcomed me when I became a minister in the RCA. He continues to encourage me through his writing. His foreword required real sacrifice to prepare when we had a short window of time. Thanks, Wes.

One of my most treasured friends is Stan Wiedeman. Stan read my earliest writing on love and offered considerable response. This led me to rewrite. Then at the end of this process he became a personal editor. His skill became evident as we pored over the finished pages searching for errors. It must be said that what errors remain are entirely my fault. Thanks, Stan. You have shown me what love looks like in a real and deeply satisfying friendship.

My longtime friend Fr. Wilbur Ellsworth shared countless meals with me to talk about divine love. He helped me find and treasure the resources of the Christian East. The late Fr. Thomas Baima helped me in ways too numerous to mention, but some of my earliest reflections on this subject with Tom gave me understanding of the Catholic tradition.

Finally, I could not write without my family. My grandsons, to whom this book is dedicated, were eager to see me finish. They asked lots of good questions. My wife, Anita, has loved me and prayed for me throughout. She is my dearest friend. Bless you for more than five decades of love and kindness. You listened to my thoughts with endless patience.

Chapter One

The Fire That Transforms

> The love of God is a consuming fire—it gladdens the soul to the point of tears by the grace of the Holy Spirit, and no earthly things can compare with it.
>
> —St. Silouan of Mount Athos

> The light of Tabor . . . is neither a physical or created light, nor yet a purely metaphorical "light of the intellect." Although non-material, it is nevertheless an objectively existent reality.
>
> —Metropolitan Archbishop Kallistos Ware

> It is he alone who has immortality and dwells in unapproachable light, whom no one has ever seen or can see.
>
> —The Apostle Paul

Most American Christians I interact with realize something is seriously amiss in the life of the church. Listen for a season and you will hear stories of personal emptiness. I believe the question that must be asked is this: "What do we need to *experience* God's love afresh?" Honestly, for many Christians it seems far too trite and humdrum to say "God is love."

The Scripture says: "Anyone united to the Lord becomes one spirit with him" (1 Cor 6:17). But reality seems to suggest this is an uncommon experience. Over the course of my fifty-plus years of ministry I have sought to know the love of God. I finally came to understand that the four Gospels of the New Testament (Matthew, Mark, Luke, and John) provide the answers I had missed. Therefore, I will try to show you how becoming "one spirit" with Christ *is the true path* to transformation. This path is the way of divine love.

Fire

In the Bible the word "fire" occurs 630 times.[1] The phrase "fire of God" (which occurs fifty-six times) captures some of the most amazing moments where God demonstrated his presence. Divine fire shows up in those places where we see mystery. For example, we read in Luke 24:32 that the disciples who walked on the Emmaus Road with the risen Jesus asked: "Were not our hearts *burning within* us while he was talking to us on the road, while he was opening the scriptures to us?" Question: Does the Spirit ever open the Scripture to you so that your heart burns within?

It seems apparent that the Scripture says that there is a love that is known and felt when our hearts *burn* with the fire of the divine presence. But this is not all. The term "light," commonly associated with God's presence, occurs in ninety-one different verses in the New Testament. Several other texts tell us that God is "a consuming fire" (cf. Heb 12:29). In the Old Testament God answered Elijah's prayer on Mount Carmel with fire (1 Kgs 18:20–40). This image of fire still holds true, even though in our time God does not seem to appear externally as a raging fire. My point is clear—the God of the Scripture is a consuming fire and often answers those who seek him by fire. But what is this fire?

Sadly, the fire of God gets a bad rap in a great deal of modern Christian thought. It seems that many see *only* the flames of Dante's images of hell when they hear this word. But what if this culture-formed image of God as fire is wrong? What if God, who is both fire and light, is really eternal love? Yes, what if?

---

1. This number comes from the use of the word in the NRSV. Other translations will of course vary. It occurs, for example, 355 times in the NLT and 364 in the NIV.

The English Mystics

There were four great English mystics in the fourteenth century, all of whom consistently spoke of God's love as fire. These four—Richard Rolle, Walter Hilton, Julian of Norwich, and the anonymous author of the classic book *The Cloud of Unknowing*—all shared an *experience of divine love* that profoundly marked the Western church in a very dark century. The written work of these four authors has now been published in excellent critical editions called "The Classics of Western Spirituality."[2] What is quite clear in these authors is that each of them expressed the core truth of God's fire as divine love.

Richard Rolle was a romantic impassioned hermit. His successor, an anonymous contemplative some have called an acute psychologist, wrote *The Cloud of Unknowing*. (This book was not published in the author's lifetime.) Walter Hilton was a gentle spiritual canon in the church while Julian was the anchoress of Norwich who authored the most famous of these four classic works: *Revelations of Divine Love*. Julian's work has been called "the finest flower of English religious literature." It was Julian who said, "Whether gracious, terrible or malignant, [all] is enwrapped in love: and is part of a world produced, not by mechanical necessity, but by passionate desire."[3] (This is a beautiful introduction to what you will read in this book.) These four writers all formed a singularly picturesque group of thinkers in the history of Christian devotion and mysticism. All four stressed the life-changing power of divine love. It is from Richard Rolle's classic, *The Fire of Love*, that I borrow the idea expressed in my title.

The Burning Bush

A marvelous turning point in the history of the Jewish people came through a vision granted to Moses recorded in Exodus 3. Moses was tending the flocks of his father-in-law when he saw a bush on fire. Yet strangely this bush was not consumed.

---

2. The Classics of Western Spirituality is a modern series published by Paulist Press. The introductions to these volumes are worth the price of each of the four books. They are academic but quite accessible. You might begin with *Revelations of Divine Love*, by Julian of Norwich, and then read the anonymous book, *The Cloud of Unknowing*.

3. Underhill, Barkway, and Lucy Menzies, eds., *Anthology of the Love of God From the Writings of Evelyn Underhill*, 47.

Several things in this account are important to see. First, Moses had to go up a mountain to draw near to God. We often climb spiritual mountains to rise above the plains of ordinary living. There will be hazards all along the way. Furthermore, like Moses we must take off our shoes and bare our feet. We stand on holy ground when we meet the fire of God. Lev Gillet, an Orthodox monk, said "The Burning Bush is a symbol of purification." But there is a supreme meaning in this encounter that we must yield ourselves to fully. "[This] is a visible expression of the very nature of God. The burning bush symbolizes the divine essence."[4] The fire of this bush is God himself. And God himself is love. Let me explain.

There are two elements to note in the burning bush. Is this fire an expression of God's anger and punishment? Though some biblical passages seem to say this, a more careful reading often shows otherwise. "The whole of the great spiritual tradition of Christianity—that of the New Testament, of the Fathers of the Church, of the saints—sees in this divine fire, in the fire of the Burning Bush, in the fire which seems to have a passion for self-communication, the incandescent charity of the Lord, the incandescence indeed of this love."[5]

Ironically, we can also see light in the transfiguration of Christ as "dazzling darkness." St. Dionysius rightly said: "The divine darkness is the inaccessible light in which God is said to dwell." The mystic Jacob Boehme put it another way: "The darkness is not the absence of light, but the terror that comes from the blinding light." Kallistos Ware concluded, "If God is said to dwell in darkness, that does not mean that there is in God any lack or privation, but that he is a fullness of glory and love beyond our comprehension."[6]

Here then is the discovery that altered my way of living more than any other: The revelation of God in the *transforming fullness of glory is beyond our comprehension*. Let that sink in. In speaking of divine love we are speaking of nothing less than the God who will never fit into our rational categories. We can speak of this love but be sure we can never exhaust it.

---

4. Gillet, *Burning Bush*, 11–12.
5. Gillet, *Burning Bush*, 12.
6. Ware, *Orthodox Way*, 128.

The Transfiguration

We get what I believe to be the best image of God's light (or fire) representing the fullness of divine love in the Gospel accounts of the transfiguration. Yes, fire does represent judgment in some places. But the light of the transfiguration represents the divine light that is the presence of God's love. "God is light; in him is no darkness at all" (1 John 1:5). "The Light, Life and Love of God—which are all the same thing really—are aspects of His Being, His Living Presence, and will be disclosed . . . to each soul according to its capacity and need."[7]

In the life of Jesus we see divine light revealed. But this fire of love was often veiled to weak human flesh.

> After six days Jesus took with him Peter, James and John the brother of James, and led them up a high mountain by themselves. There he was transfigured before them. His face shone like the sun, and his clothes became as white as the light. Just then there appeared before them Moses and Elijah, talking with Jesus.
>
> Peter said to Jesus, "Lord, it is good for us to be here. If you wish, I will put up three shelters—one for you, one for Moses and one for Elijah."
>
> While he was still speaking, a bright cloud covered them, and a voice from the cloud said, "This is my Son, whom I love; with him I am well pleased. Listen to him!"
>
> When the disciples heard this, they fell facedown to the ground, terrified. But Jesus came and touched them. "Get up," he said. "Don't be afraid." When they looked up, they saw no one except Jesus. (Matt 17:1–9; cf. Mark 9:2–10; Luke 9:28–36)

Students of the Scripture recognize that there is no direct reference to the transfiguration in John's Gospel. This seems odd until you read more carefully. Why? The very first paragraph in the fourth Gospel says "we have seen his glory" (John 1:14). But when? The word glory is *doxa*, a word which is almost universally recognized as a tangible manifestation of the divinity of Christ. This is exactly what the three disciples saw in the transfiguration. There are three events in Scripture that profoundly accentuate Christ's divinity: the transfiguration, the resurrection, and the ascension. In the Christian East these three are represented in icons (drawings of holy truth) that suggest that all three of them are saving events made visible. An intense interest in a theology of light breaks

---

7. Underhill, Barkaway, and Menzies, eds., *Anthology of the Love of God*, 43.

through with deep clarity in John. "I am the light of the world. Whoever follows me will never walk in darkness but will have the light of life." (John 8:12). John clearly links divine love with divine light.

Thus the divine light, seen by the three disciples who accompanied Jesus up the mountain, is nothing less than the "uncreated energies of God."[8] This light was neither physical nor created. And it was not purely metaphorical, as in the phrase the "light of the intellect." *It is nonmaterial but nothing less than an objectively existent reality.* Clearly this kind of language employs both paradox and symbolism. This is perhaps the most glorious demonstration we have of what it means to see the mutual infusion of both divinity and humanity in Christ. Thus divinity and humanity are seen in Jesus as divine light shining through his person. This is what the Orthodox East understood by a *theology of light*.

In this account the three disciples encountered the Trinity, revealed as blinding light. Notice, the Father speaks, the Son is present and being spoken to, and the Spirit is revealed in the form of the cloud. Both the fire and the cloud are joined together in one glorious revelation. *Here union with God is expressed as a continual transformation into the very likeness of God as Trinity, clearly showing that salvation is more than a ticket to heaven when we die. Trinitarian salvation is a radical transformation.* Peter, one of the three apostles on the mountain, worked out a theology rooted in this transfiguration experience.

> By his divine power, God has given us everything we need for living a godly life. We have received all of this by coming to know him, the one who called us to himself by means of his *marvelous glory and excellence*. And because of his glory and excellence, he has given us great and precious promises. These are the promises that enable you *to share his divine nature and escape the world's corruption caused by human desires.* (2 Peter 1:3–5)

This text refers to the light and fire of the Spirit's work in us as *deification*, an idea that has taken me years to talk about intelligently. Peter says we *are enabled to share God's divine nature*. But why does this matter for my theme of transforming divine love?

---

8. This term "energies" was used in Eastern Orthodox theology. God's essence was called *ousia*, "all that subsists by itself and which has not its being in another," and is distinct from his energies (*energeia* in Greek), or his activities as actualized in the world. The *ousia* of God is God as God is. The energies of God are what we see God doing. His energies are sometimes identified with his glory, his grace, the uncreated light. The energies are also God's actions of doing things like healing, miracles, forgiveness of sins, the power in the sacraments, etc.

Being divine, the uncreated energies surpass our human powers of description; and so, in terming these energies "light," we are inevitably employing the language of "sign" and symbol. Not that the energies themselves are *merely* symbolical. They genuinely exist, *but cannot be described in words*; in referring to them as "light" we use the least misleading term, but our language is not to be interpreted literally.[9]

This image of fire and light is revealed in the Bible again and again. Here, in Matthew 17, the image comes to be a dramatic revelation of the grace and love seen in Christ Jesus. Vladimir Lossky (1903–1958), an influential Russian theologian, was not entirely using metaphorical language when he said: "The fire of grace, kindled in the hearts of Christians by the Holy Spirit, makes them shine like tapers before the Son of God."[10] St. Maximus the Great said: "The body is deified at the same time as the soul."[11]

Not being taught how and why the transfiguration kindled this fire in me was a great loss.[12] For decades I read the transfiguration text as something that only happened to Jesus in history, thus it had little to do with my inner-self being *transformed by the fire of love*. I now understand I am being transfigured/transformed every time I receive the bread and wine of the Lord's Supper. (While we debate among ourselves as Christians just what Jesus meant by "this is my body . . . this is my blood," many Protestants, though not all for sure, fail to see the mystery of Christ's *presence*.) A modern Orthodox theologian puts this memorably: "The relationship of the church and God has been described in countless texts. In the Song of Songs it is described as a relationship of deep love. God may be above all passions and necessities, but we recognize in him only one strong passion: his intense love for humankind."[13]

There are many examples of God's fire and light coming through people who walked with God. When Moses descended from Mt. Sinai his face shone with brilliance. No one could gaze upon him so a veil was

---

9. Ware, *Orthodox Way*, 127.

10. Ware, *Orthodox Way*, 127.

11. Ware, *Orthodox Way*, 127.

12. The almost complete repudiation of symbol and metaphor in Protestant readings of the Bible caused me to see this account as a "one-off" historical event that had no bearing on anyone except these three disciples. I situated this text in the passion week story (which is correct) and then left it there. Every aspect of the divine drama, thus the transfiguration, resurrection, ascension and Pentecost, mystically become our *real experience* in the present if we partake in the nature of Christ.

13. Andreopoulos, *This is My Beloved Son*, 131.

constructed in order that they could talk with him (Exod 34:29–35). In *The Sayings of the Desert Fathers* we read about a disciple looking through the window of Abba Arsenius's room only to see the old man looking like a "flame of fire." (As rare as this type of experience may be it was understood and accepted in the church long *before* the Reformation.)

The Holy Spirit and Fire

John the Baptist, who came to announce the Messiah's arrival, said of the Savior: "I baptize you with water for repentance, but the one who is coming after me is more powerful than I, and I am not worthy to carry his sandals. He will baptize you with the Holy Spirit and fire" (Matt 3:11). Thus the Holy Spirit *is* the flame of God, the fire of divine love. The author of the book of Acts says: "Divided tongues, as of fire, appeared among them, and a tongue rested on each of them (Acts 2:3). When the Spirit came upon the early disciples they saw "tongues of fire" resting on one another.

God not only consumes our being through the fire of his limitless love but the Holy Trinity baptizes us "with the Holy Spirit and fire." The word translated "baptize" means *to submerge,* thus this is a promise that Jesus will *submerge us into the fire of God*. But this fire will not harm you. Why? God *is* love. This fire will completely transform you from the inside out. It will empower you to change by captivating your entire being. This is nothing less than what happened on the Mount of Transfiguration. This is the meaning of the burning bush.

This image of fire is the way many of the greatest saints in history have understood the love of God. I use it because divine love is not a sweet, gentle, passive spirit but rather a love that powerfully cleanses and restores. This love is not soft and weak. If you miss this then most of what I say will not make a real difference in your life.

"God is fire. God is love. God is a self-propagating emotional power, a fire that shares itself. In saying that God is a fire of love we are certainly stating a truth that plays havoc with many of our ideas, in fact almost all of our ideas."[14]

This is the transforming fire of divine love.

---

14. Gillet, *Burning Bush*, 12.

Chapter Two

An Astonishing Statement

> Among all the influences that contribute to our development
> none is more important than our idea of God.
> —Louis Evely

> Only Christianity . . . defines itself as the religion of
> love, [since Christianity] alone has made love the
> dominant principle in all areas of dogma.
> —Irving Singer

> Without love, life becomes a more or less tolerable
> descent into death. To give up on love is also to
> give up on the world and each other.
> —Norman Wirzba

CHRISTIAN THINKERS HAVE UNIVERSALLY agreed on one core truth about the character of God: "God is love" (1 John 4:8). The Scots-American philosopher-theologian Geddes MacGregor (1909–1998) called this text "an astonishing utterance," saying "[it] has captured the hearts of devout men and women everywhere and has even occasionally tempered the opposition of some skeptics."[1] For good reason the famous Swiss Reformed theologian Emil Brunner(1889–1966) called this statement "daring." In my estimation that is putting it quite mildly. This claim is either outrageous or astonishing. Trite it surely cannot be.

I submit then that "God is love" is the most astonishing statement in all the Bible.

Yet too few Christians see it this way. We must have a problem! My intention is to expose the sources of this problem and offer some credible and consistent ways for understanding and entering into the experience of "God is love."

Though these *exact* words—"God is love"—occur only three times in the entire New Testament, the truth behind them is widely recognized as the reason for creation itself. "Divine love lies at the foundation of the universe, it governs the world, and it will lead the world to that glorious outcome when it will be entirely consumed by the Godhead."[2]

Far too few Christians seem astonished by God's love. Go figure. Actually, we seem to have lost the ability to be astonished! But this question remains: What does it mean to confess and live the truth that God *is* love?

This biblical affirmation led the late American philosopher Irving Singer, author of a massive three-volume work titled *The Nature of Love*, to say that Christianity *alone* has made love the dominant principle in all theology.[3] I believe Singer is right. But why? Jesus of Nazareth "explodes all the categories and classifications we use to describe who is 'in' or 'out,' worthy or unworthy, because [his] reach is infinite, encompassing everything that is."[4]

This much I know without doubt: Jesus loves me because the narrative of the Bible tells me so. I have come to know this love in a deeply personal way because of the transforming fire of the Holy Spirit.

The Character of God

At the outset we need to see that it is not enough to merely believe in God. We must *know* the God we believe in. There are many views of God that

---

1. MacGregor, *He Who Lets Us Be*, 3.
2. Alfayev, *Spiritual World of Isaac the Syrian*, 37.
3. Singer, *Nature of Love*, 159.
4. Wirzba, *Way of Love*, 3.

cause far too many Christians to be confused about who God is. What particularly confuses many are the various metaphors used to describe God and his actions. Some of these metaphors actually have the power to shape our lives in some very negative ways.

In his autobiography the American journalist and critic Thomas Matthews, a pastor's kid, wrote:

> Try as I may, I cannot altogether shake off my habitual awe of the church nor completely disassociate it from the far more fearful God to whom the church makes its ritual obeisance. I still think of God—no, not think, but apprehend, as I was trained as a child to envision him—as a watchful, vengeful, enormous, omniscient policeman, instantly aware of the slightest tinge of irreverence in my innermost thought, always ready to pounce if I curse, if I mention him in anger, fun or mere habit (though with ominous patience he might hold his hand for a time). . . . But how can that kind of fear of that kind of God be the beginning of wisdom?[5]

As you read I pray that "God is love" will come into sharper focus. I further hope that you will begin to see how this profound truth *alone* can draw you to God and keep you in the transforming fire of his presence.

To begin we must construct a simple foundation. Divine truth can only be grasped when we make an honest attempt to deepen our understanding. I am fully persuaded that divine love is the sure foundation upon which we can build lasting faith. Yet here the pursuit to understand God's love often breaks down. We reason: How can God *be* love and yet allow so much disaster in the world? Or we think, if God is the Creator, *and* God is eternal love, then why does God not intervene to stop tragedies? These thorny questions, sometimes leading to what we call a theodicy (a way to understand the problem of evil), perplex both theologies and theologians. (For that matter these questions puzzle all three monotheistic traditions in particular.) Christians ask, "Who does God *really* love? Only those who choose to love him? Or only those God chooses to love? Or does God love all persons, both good and bad? Does God love only those who believe in Jesus or does he love the entire world? Does God ever *stop* loving those who *refuse* his love?" (We will soon see that the answers to such questions, offered by sincere Christians, profoundly differ.)

Further, how can we say that God *is* love when it seems that God appears, at least in the Old Testament, to be a stern judge who seems filled

---

5. Matthews, *Under the Influence*, 343.

with wrath and anger against all ungodliness and ungodly people? These, and a myriad of related questions, have fueled a long-standing debate about the *meaning* of God's love. In the context of this debate modern people have drifted further and further into ways of coping with life that do not seriously consider the meaning of divine love. To my mind this is a great tragedy!

But let's be honest. Love has never been easy to grasp.

> [Love] has always been a contested and fragile power, vulnerable to multiple forms of misunderstanding and abuse. Discovering the truth of love and the trustworthiness of Christianity's expressions must, therefore, go hand in hand. For too long, too many Christians have acted as if by simply reading scripture and adopting the name "Christian" they have been inoculated with the equivalent of a "love gene."[6]

The History of Love

Carter Lindberg, in a history of the place of love in Western culture, shows how love in all its guises has always been debated. He says this subject spans the depths and complexity of an often elusive topic. To demonstrate this Lindberg sketches the lives, words, works and movements associated with love. He interacts with theologians and philosophers such as Augustine, Abelard, Luther, and Feuerbach. He traces numerous intellectual and theological movements like Romanticism and the Protestant Reformation. He engages with both the mystics and the pietists, all the while seeking to show *how* love has developed in our culture.[7]

At the end of Lindberg's book he references how the famous apologist C. S. Lewis understood divine love. You may remember that Lewis wrote a popular book titled *The Four Loves*. (This book is often cited by modern pastors and teachers.) Lewis said God's love is pure *agape*.[8] (Interestingly enough Lewis never used the word *agape* in the book.) Many still argue that this one Greek word represents the true *distinctiveness* of

---

6. Wirzba, *Way of Love*, 3.

7. Lindberg, *Love: A Brief History Through Western Christianity*.

8. It is often argued that *agapé* is the word of choice to say God's love means it is always self-giving love. Lewis said *eros* is about making promises while *agape* keeps them. The third Greek word for love is *philia*, which means affectionate regard, friendship. Modern scholarship has a much broader view of how all three of these Greek words can be rightly used for the love of God.

God's love in the Bible. But Lindberg shows how four common Greek words for love have all been frequently used in positive ways for the love of God—especially *eros* and *agape*. These two words repeatedly inform dialogues and debates about divine love. (The other two Greek words for love are *storge* and *phileo*, the latter also having an important role in understanding God's love, as we shall see.) Lewis argued that these four Greek words employ both Hellenistic and biblical sources to inform our conceptions of love. Lindberg reasons that both *eros* and *agape* reveal what the Scripture means by love when it speaks directly about God. Lindberg writes that he gained a new "appreciation" for C. S. Lewis's thinking by reading his Introduction to *The Four Loves*. Here Lewis wrote: "I cannot now deny the name *love* to need-love. Every time I have tried to think the thing out along those lines I have ended in puzzles and contradictions. The reality is more complicated than I supposed."[9] If the single most often quoted popular writer on the meaning of God's love, and the four Greek words used for love in ancient literature and the New Testament, says this subject is "more complicated than I supposed," surely we are wise to reject simplistic solutions in our quest to understand divine love. For this reason I hope that what I write will be clear without being reductionistic or simplistic.[10]

Lewis's statement that understanding love in the Bible is far "more complicated than I supposed" sums up my own experience. I first read C. S. Lewis in college when I took an English course titled: "Modern Christian Myth."[11] Initially I accepted the widely held view that *agape* was the way to *distinguish* God's love from all other loves. I even preached this idea. But the more I thought I understood God's love the more I was forced to rethink the character of God and the various words for love in the Bible.[12] I now see that divine love is indeed a gift but this gift draws us into the experience of love, an experience that creates a deep relationship with the giver by appealing to our *desire* for a good life. It is this desire

9. Lewis, *Four Loves*, 10.

10. I argue that all four Greek words, in different ways, can be used to describe the love of God.

11. This course, taught by the well-known Lewis scholar Clyde Kilby, included the works of Lewis, Dorothy Sayers, J. R. R. Tolkien, Charles Williams, and George MacDonald. By "myth" the professor did not mean these writers told untruths, but rather they used "myth" to tell the Christian story.

12. It is important to not isolate the New Testament from the Old Testament. If God is love then he is love in all the Bible, though, as we shall see, there are different nuances regarding love in the varied texts of the Bible.

that leads us to know *both* the gift and the giver. This gift ultimately leads to friendship.[13] Yet it still surprises me every time I read authors who think they have understood God's love by appealing singularly to this word *agape*. Biblical love cannot be mastered through word studies! In fact, love cannot be mastered at all. Love can only be embraced and lived. Love must become the life-changing reality that fills you with all the fullness of God, the God who burns with passionate love.

Jesus Loves Me!

The twentieth century's most highly regarded Protestant theologian was undoubtedly Karl Barth (1886–1968). When Professor Barth visited America in 1962 he spoke at the Rockefeller Chapel on the campus of the University of Chicago. After his lecture, during a Q&A time, a student asked Barth if he could *summarize* his life's work in theology. Barth reportedly said: "Yes, I can. In the words of a song I learned at my mother's knee: 'Jesus loves me, this I know, for the Bible tells me so.'" There has been some debate about Barth being asked this question and giving this answer but, after some research, I am persuaded this response really did happen. The great theologian summarized his massive theological output with a children's chorus.

But Does God Love *Me*?

Karl Barth took "God is love" seriously in his massive theology of God. *With Barth I submit that "God is love" is undeniably the most stunning statement regarding God in the entire biblical canon.* We are not just told that God loves, which is true, but that God *is* love. Love is not just one *part* of God's nature, it is *God's nature. Love is who God is.* Love is "the inner dynamic of God."[14]

What this means is this: God, who is one in essence and three in person, freely loves you and me out of the very center of his divine being. Love is the window through which we see the reality of how God should

---

13. Jesus says: "I do not call you servants any longer, because the servant does not know what the master is doing, but I have called you *friends*, because I have made known to you everything that I have heard from my Father" (John 15:15). We will examine this more directly in a later chapter.

14. Grenz, *Theology for the Community of God*, 92.

be understood. "It is out of God's "goodness and loving kindness [that] our Savior appeared . . . [to] save us" (Titus 3:4–5). After a lifetime of reading, praying, and contemplating this divine mystery I sincerely hope I can show you *how* this is true.

Understand that I am using the word *nature* in a specific sense. It refers to the inherent character or basic constitution of a person. The word *essence* could also be used here to describe God as love. What do I mean by the word *essence*? The Merriam-Webster Online Dictionary says the word means "the properties or attributes by means of which something can be placed in its proper class or identified as being what it is." In this sense God's essence is love.

Jesus really does love you!

If love is who God is, then are we not warranted to say that God never acts in unloving ways? (Read this question several times and realize that I am fully aware that many Christians will disagree.) While I could cite numerous passages to support my claim I will give you just one statement from Jesus.

> You have heard that it was said, "You shall love your neighbor and hate your enemy." But I say to you: Love your enemies and pray for those who persecute you, so that you may be children of your Father in heaven, for he makes his sun rise on the evil and on the good and sends rain on the righteous and on the unrighteous. For if you love those who love you, what reward do you have? Do not even the tax collectors do the same? And if you greet only your brothers and sisters, what more are you doing than others? Do not even the gentiles do the same? Be perfect, therefore, as your heavenly Father is perfect. (Matt 5:43–48)

Jesus plainly says the Father provides sunshine for the evil and the unrighteous, thus God commands us to love our enemies and pray for them. But why? *Because God loves them.* We see this same expression spoken by Jesus from the cross: "Father, forgive them, for they do not know what they are doing" (Luke 23:34). If we are to be like God then we too must love our enemies. Therefore, it seems self-evident that love is central to the entire being of Jesus. For this reason those who follow Jesus must seek to love in the way God loves. But such love is not remotely possible *without* a growing understanding and experience of God's love for us. (This same idea of love and mercy toward our enemies can also be seen in Luke 6:35–36.)

Love and the Creeds

It has been rightly noted that the word "love" does not occur in any of the early creeds of the so-called undivided church. Yet when all is said and done I stand by this thesis: *Divine love is the most fundamental of all the articles of the Christian faith.* To emphasize the identification of God with love sees "God's self-revealing and self-giving action as Love, with a capital L. Only by surrendering to Love and cooperation with it can we hope to understand it more fully."[15] Paul prayed for believers in first-century Ephesus that "Christ may dwell in your hearts through faith, as you are being rooted and grounded in love" (Eph 3:17).

Here then is my goal: to encourage you to continually give your life to divine love and cooperate with it, through the Spirit's power, in every way possible so you may increasingly be transformed into the image of Christ.

Time and time again I have found that the only way to understand and experience love is through *surrender*. (The word "surrender" has so many negative connotations in our culture yet, rightly understood, this word means that in Christ we surrender not to power but to eternal love.) This may sound easy at first but I assure you it is not. It will cost you everything. Jesus said, "If any wish to come after me, let them deny themselves and take up their cross daily and follow me" (Luke 9:23). The way of divine love demands sacrifice but the end is always worth the journey!

Popular evangelical writer David Jeremiah rightly says "the momentous task of describing God's love. . . . [caused me to see] that when I have said everything I can possibly say about the love of God, I will barely have touched it."[16] I share this sense of wonder and awe when I stand back and gaze at this tallest of all of God's mountains of divine revelation.

God is love. He always has been and always will be!

God Proves His Love for Us

The apostle Paul concurs with John's affirmation that *God is love*. "But God proves his love for us in that while we still were sinners Christ died

---

15. Kelly, *God Is Love*, 1.
16. Jeremiah, *God Loves You*, 6.

for us" (Rom 5:8). In the verses that follow in Romans 8 Paul demonstrates that love "eliminates any fear concerning a future angry judgment. We can know that God is just not like this. Hence a scary future scenario of raging punishment is not merely avoidable: It is false."[17]

But does this mean that love cannot involve anger and judgment? Any relationship, especially one where love is so intense and real, would not be a relationship of love *without* these dimensions. I have come to believe that a number of early theologians were correct to see that anger and judgment were never intended to *destroy. The design of this divine anger and judgment is not intended* to reject us but rather to bring us into relationship. Much as good parents judge and correct out of love, our heavenly Father does the same. I think theologian Douglas A. Campbell grasps this clearly: "The nature of God is revealed definitively by the death of the Son on the cross for us at the behest of the Father and the Spirit."[18] Thus the nature of God, revealed in Jesus Christ, is love.

We shall come to the subject of the cross and the Trinity in later chapters but for now we should pause to see that it is the Father who offered up his beloved Son for us. *This was all for love.* God's Son obediently carried out the mission of his Father by his death on the cross. *This was all because of love.* The mystery of our great salvation is thus rooted in this unique love story that we can know through the gift of the Holy Spirit.

The apostle Paul concluded his great praise of love (1 Cor 13) with these familiar words:

> For now we see only a reflection, as in a mirror, but then we will see face to face. Now I know only in part; then I will know fully, even as I have been fully known. And now faith, hope, and love remain, these three, and the greatest of these is love. (1 Cor 13:12–13)

Conclusion

So we begin here. The mystery of God's love is not a problem to be solved but an inexhaustible reality that we must actively receive if we are to continually draw near to God. We were created to experience divine love. God cannot be *discovered* through logic or science, though both have a powerful role to play in modern life. Faith requires deeper thought but true faith

17. Campbell, *Pauline Dogmatics*, 55.
18. Campbell, *Pauline Dogmatics*, 55–56.

is not mastering words or Bible verses. True faith is an inner *confidence* grounded in what we can only see (perceive) dimly (1 Cor 13:12).

Thus the apostle gives us a way to experience life with profound confidence in the love of God. I now believe that the Christian must always be challenged to strive for this deeper understanding of the love of God. "Though what it means to 'predicate' love of God remains something of a mystery, this has not impeded its use in human affairs. . . . The mere frequency of the term's use, however, stands in inverse proportion to its meaningfulness."[19]

The Scottish minister George Matheson (1842–1906) knew both great love and great loss. At age twenty he began to lose his eyesight. He was studying theology to become a minister, which he determined to do anyway. He also planned to marry his sweetheart but she told him she could not go through life with a blind husband. Several years later Matheson was a guest at a wedding where his former fiancée was present. That evening his heart was broken again. He went back to his room and wrote a hymn that we still sing in many churches. (He never wrote another hymn, saying he was not able to do this type of writing. He added that he wrote this hymn in three or four minutes! He did, however, write dozens of books.) Clearly he experienced the truth of God's love and *lived it* in the deepest recesses of his broken heart. We should strive, no less, for the same.

> I yield my flickering torch to thee
> My heart restores its borrowed ray
> That in thy sunshine's blaze its day
> May brighter, fairer be.
> Oh joy that seekest me through pain
> I cannot close my heart to thee
> I trace the rainbow through the rain
> And feel the promise is not vain
> That morn shall tearless be.
> Oh cross that liftest up my head
> I dare not ask to fly from thee
> I lay in dust's life's glory dead
> And from the ground there blossoms red
> Life that shall endless be.

---

19. Vanhoozer, ed. *Nothing Greater, Nothing Better*, 1–2.

Chapter Three

The Bible Tells Me So

> Christian love is not the world's last word about itself—it is
> God's final word about himself, and so about the world.
>
> —Hans Urs von Balthasar

> Love is not merely an outward mark and symbol of His
> presence, but is His very self in action in our world.
>
> —John Baillie

As we've seen, the New Testament plainly says God is love. This statement itself is not debatable. But understanding it will require careful reading joined with an experience that invites us into deep transformation. Views about divine love range widely over contested understanding. I invite you to open your heart and mind to reconsider what you've been taught about God. If you are wrong about God's nature as love then the consequences are considerable.

The late Old Testament scholar Terence E. Fretheim aptly noted, "All too often the sole focus of the ministry of the church is on whether one believes in God. Insufficient attention has been given to the kind of God in whom one believes, often with disastrous results.... The question of the kind of God in whom one believes is not only important, it is crucial. It is a question of images. Metaphors matter."[1] Hold this idea in your mind as you read. Hopefully you will see again and again that metaphors do matter. Think about it. How else could we understand a God who is beyond us and, at the same time, passionately in love with us? But the problem is that so many misapply the metaphors and thus misunderstand the Scriptures.

Fretheim shows how multiple atrocities, from the Inquisition to Jonestown, have been committed in the name of God. Moreover, to define God primarily in terms of activity can get one into profound difficulties. The God served at Jonestown was a creator and a redeemer. David Koresh, and his Branch Davidian followers in Waco, read and studied the Bible daily. They believed the Bible was inspired and perfect. They also believed that God had a clear plan for them which they saw by reading the Bible.[2]

The late professor Geddes MacGregor wrote on the flyleaf of a book he authored that the love of God is an invitation: "To those who are willing to use their minds as rigorously in their religion as in their other concerns."[3] You may disagree with some of my conclusions, even by appealing to specific Bible texts, but I urge you to use your mind and keep learning. Consider that your assumptions may actually be wrong. This fundamental question remains: "What does the Bible actually teach us about God's love?"

The philosophical theologian Paul Tillich said theology ought to satisfy two basic needs: to state the truth of the Christian message and to interpret that truth for each generation.[4] In this spirit of doing good theology my goal is to faithfully *represent* the truth of Christian faith and to *interpret* this truth well. Be honest. We all *interpret* the Scripture so we all should be willing to listen and learn afresh. We should acknowledge that the harshest representations of Christian truth actually rely on texts and stories in the Bible, texts that are broadly misinterpreted.

Where then should we begin our journey? My advice is simple: begin where the Scriptures begin, with the God who *is* love. When you start with divine love you will see that the kind of love that describes God's

---

1. Fretheim, *Suffering of God*, 1–2.

2. The Branch Davidians were an offshoot of the Seventh-day Adventists. Adventists are rightly viewed as a denomination that is Christian. Many Christians are too quick to use the word "cult" to explain away things they reject.

3. MacGregor, *He Who Lets Us Be*, v.

4. Tillich, *Systematic Theology*, 1:3.

being is at the center of the biblical narratives. We will also see that this love is intensely *relational*. God loves us and seeks relationship with us. Let me be abundantly clear—divine love is never an abstraction. It is not a force. God loves specific persons, persons he created. God doesn't just love the world in a broadly benevolent sense. He *loves* the whole world in a deeply personal sense because he created it out of love and continues to intensely care for it because of love. His love is not detached and never stoical. It is passionate and intense.

Can I Know God Is Love?

How then do I know that God is eternal love? First, I must put myself in a disposition of poverty. By this I do not mean economic deprivation. You will discover, when you pray for God to reveal himself to you, that his answers will likely surprise you. The indispensable disposition we must cultivate is beautifully seen in the Virgin Mary's response to the Spirit's telling her she would give birth to the Messiah: "Here am I, the servant of the Lord; let it be with me according to your word" (Luke 1:38). She joyfully gives herself to God.

Second, we must *not* adopt philosophical formulas as "proofs" for divine love. This approach, rooted in what is called "natural theology," sometimes turns proofs into rationalistic notions that can actually hinder us from *knowing* God.[5] What I understand about divine love has been fully *revealed* in Jesus Christ: "I am the way and the truth and the life. No one comes to the Father except through me" (John 14:6). We do not figure God out and then discover that God is love. John's statement about divine love means the fundamental ontological[6] statement of the divine nature is clear: "God is love." The one God who exists from everlasting to everlasting is love, *personal holy love*.

Finally, we must believe that God exists and that he has spoken. When the disciples heard the risen Lord they said, "Were not our hearts

---

5. Natural theology is based on reason and science, thus on observed facts. We can learn a great deal from natural theology but it is doubtful that we would come to know that God is love from this approach. Revealed theology is based on both the Scriptures and Christian experience. This will be our anchor in the ensuing chapters.

6. Ontology refers to claims that are made about the nature of being and existence. One dictionary of theology says: "You can sum up ontology by the commonsense observation, 'If it ain't one thing, it's another.'" It considers when a difference is a matter of essence or appearance. A simple theological example is the difference between human beings and God." See Jacobson, *Crazy Talk*.

burning within us while he was talking to us on the road, while he was opening the scriptures to us" (Luke 24:32). When we experience divine love in this way we burst forth into praise. "God alone could love in this way . . . God alone could forgive in this way. Read the whole Gospel. It is on this word that one must make up their mind for or against Christ, on a certain impression he has made on his heart, and it is overwhelming."[7]

This discovery of love is not a "leap in the dark." *The knowledge of God comes through divine self-disclosure.* The history of Israel shows how the covenant people knew the promises God made to Abraham. They learned of the revelation of the sacred name of God to Moses and of the deliverance of Israel from bondage in Egypt. They celebrated the giving of the law and the words of the prophets. These events all showed them that God had revealed himself. In the New Testament God was finally revealed in the life, death, and resurrection of Jesus Christ. Jesus is God's Word incarnate; the one through whom God took the initiative to freely make his identity known. All of this is interpersonal, not merely a set of facts. We get to know God in much the same way as we get to know other persons, by knowing who God is and by seeing what he does.

Relations and Relationship

I find the truth of knowing and loving God developed beautifully in the words of St. Silouan: "My brother is my life." At the core of the Christian belief is this astounding revelation that God is the one and the three that we experience in living with others. *This means that Trinity is the revelation of the very character of our human existence.* This further means that the word "relationship" describes more than a meeting for a meal or helping one another out now and then.

One of the most basic mistakes Christians make about God occurs when they conceive of him as an object. God is never an object. He is one, yet he is three distinct and inseparable persons. Baptist theologian Roger Olson captures this point.

> Behind this imagery God [who is three distinct persons] is "alive, dynamic, ever active and moving." In other words, God cannot be pinned down like a dead butterfly in a display box. This is one way of saying "God is spirit." Unlike created things, God cannot be measured, dissected, analyzed, defined or controlled. Yes,

---

7. Evely, *Religion for Our Time*, 17.

God is personal. But not in the same way a human is personal. A human being is also an object.[8]

For the patristic writers of the early church these words *"relation"* and *"relationship"* were expressions of mutual indwelling; thus indwelling is the Bible's unique way of saying *this* exists because *that* exists and that both *exist* in one another. (We will explore this in chapter 12.) Simply put, we do *not* create relationships. We *are* relationships and we perceive this and pay attention to it or we do not.[9]

The Apostolic Gospel of Love

The clearest articulation we have of God's nature as love occurs in the fourth chapter of the First Letter of John. It is worth reading this whole portion of Scripture.

> Beloved, let us love one another, because love is from God; everyone who loves is born of God and knows God. Whoever does not love does not know God, for *God is love*. God's love was revealed among us in this way: God sent his only Son into the world so that we might live through him. In this is love, not that we loved God but that he loved us and sent his Son to be the atoning sacrifice for our sins. Beloved, since God loved us so much, we also ought to love one another. No one has ever seen God; if we love one another, God lives in us, and his love is perfected in us.
>
> By this we know that we abide in him and he in us, because he has given us of his Spirit. And we have seen and do testify that the Father has sent his Son as the Savior of the world. God abides in those who confess that Jesus is the Son of God, and they abide in God. So we have known and believe the love that God has for us.
>
> *God is love*, and those who abide in love abide in God, and God abides in them. Love has been perfected among us in this: that we may have boldness on the day of judgment, because as he is, so are we in this world. There is no fear in love, but perfect love casts out fear; for fear has to do with punishment,

---

8. Olson, *Finding God in the Shack*, 32–33. *The Shack* is a controversial book that Olson believes is a good book with minor flaws. I have come to agree with this critique. I believe the reason this popular book caught the attention of many is because God is presented by the author as a "dynamic, ever active" personal being of love.

9. Freeman, "Alone—You Are Not."

and whoever fears has not reached perfection in love. (1 John 4:7–18, my italics)

Observe several vital truths here that reveal who God is.

1. Love is *from* God.
2. Everyone who loves is *born* of God and *knows* God.
3. Everyone who does *not* love does *not know* God.
4. We *know* God's love *because* he sent his Son into the world.
5. The Son of God is an *atoning sacrifice* for our sin. He died for love.
6. Since God loved us this much we *ought* to love one another.
7. No one has "seen" God but if we love then his *love lives in us*. Simply put, God lives in us since he is love.
8. Those who confess that Jesus is the Son of God *abide in God*, thus in God's love.
9. *God is love.*
10. Love has been perfected among us so that we might have *boldness* on the day of judgment, because as he is, *so are we in this world*.
11. There is *no fear* in God's love. Why? The fear referenced here has to do with punishment. If we reach perfection (full maturity) we reach the place of no fear.

Love Is the Touchstone—John 3:16

Some of you may recall seeing a man wearing a multicolored wig, at American sports events. He would strategically place himself in the crowd to be in full view of the TV cameras. He held up a sign which simply said: "3:16." Multitudes had no idea what this meant. The famous football star Tim Tebow did something similar when he placed this 3:16 reference on his eye black (the strip underneath a player's eyes to deflect the light) before a national championship football game. It has been said that after that game ninety million hits were recorded by people looking up 3:16. Millions of words have been written about 3:16, a single verse in the Gospel of John. I learned this verse as a small boy, taught it to my own children, and now teach it to my grandchildren. But why?

Christian faith rightly understood that Christianity cannot exist without divine love. *This is not a secondary doctrine.* It is not my hobby horse. Yet I was in the pastoral ministry nearly twenty years before I *preached* John 3:16. (I am not entirely sure why but part of the reason may become apparent as you read my story.) When I finally did preach this remarkable verse I devoted five sermons to it in order to exhaust what I wanted to say. But exhaust the love of God I never did!

After I left the pastorate in 1992, to lead a mission that took me to churches large and small across America, as well as to countries in Europe, South America, and Asia, I began to preach John 3:16 again and again. I never felt I could preach it well but this never stopped me from trying. This became the touchstone for my mission.

But Does God Love the Whole Cosmos?[10]

Here is this oft-quoted verse, along with the verse that follows it:

> For God so loved the world that he gave his only Son, so that everyone who believes in him may not perish but may have eternal life. Indeed, God did not send the Son into the world to condemn the world but in order that the world might be saved through him. (John 3:16–17)

What do these few words mean? Does God love *all* people or only *some*? Does God love the entire world, by which I mean the whole cosmos that lives in sin and unbelief? If God sent the Son into the world, what does "send" mean when verse 17 adds that God did *not* send his Son to *condemn* the world but rather to *save* it? How should we understand God's nature if he *loves our world*? To ask this another way: Who is God in himself? *You might think that defining the person of God is easy but I assure you nothing is further from reality.* It is here that problems arise, especially when we try to explain God by using our favorite theological categories.

---

10. In John the word *world* is from the Greek word *kosmos*. It is used seventy-eight times in the Gospel of John and twenty-four times in his epistles. It refers to sinful humanity arrayed in opposition against God. Simply put, God loves all fallen and broken people.

The Bible's Golden Text

John's Gospel says more about God's love than any of the other three Gospels. In fact, love reaches a glorious crescendo here in John 3:16. For this reason John 3:16 has rightly been called "the golden text" of the Bible.

Simply put—John says salvation is God's love story. (Remember, divine love is intensely personal and relational.) "God so loved the world." The tense of this verb "love" implies a supreme act. As we saw above in John's Epistle this gift is underscored by these words: "God's love was revealed among us in this way: God sent his only Son into the world so that we might live through him" (1 John 4:9). Thus we are given the perfect example of the *how* of God's love, expressing itself in both the incarnation and death of Jesus. It is apparent in the Gospels (as we saw earlier in Matthew 5) that God's love is his nature. He loves his enemies and sends blessings upon them. This is who God is in his being! I submit that any theology of God should begin here and move forward by explaining other texts.

I still remember the late African American evangelist Tom Skinner saying in chapel at Wheaton College in 1969: "If John said God so loved the world . . . and then stopped there . . . I would say to him: 'So what?' But he says so much more when he adds, 'that he gave.'" The late Catholic biblical scholar Raymond E. Brown underscored what the evangelist meant: "The classical use of this construction is for the purpose of stressing the reality of the result: that he actually *gave* the only Son."[11] Thus it is for good reason John 3:16 is widely viewed as the *classic summary* of the central message of divine love. God gave his "only" Son. Why? Because God *loves* the world. God's giving is radical, unreserved, risky, and painful.[12]

God's Design for the World

The verse following John 3:16 *should not be omitted if we are to understand God's purpose in creating and loving the whole world."* Indeed, "God did not send the Son into the world to condemn the world but in order that

---

11. Brown, *Gospel of John, I–XII*, 134.

12. I will not address all the biblical texts and issues that have often been cited to suggest that divine love revealed in Christ cannot be the central story of the Bible. In a small book aimed at non-scholars this cannot be done. I am fully aware of these texts and the arguments developed in them.

the world might be saved through him" (3:17). "The accent falls on God's initiative and love for the world. . . . [The] Father and Son are always one in John, and the salvation gift is the self-donation of God-Jesus."[13] God gives his only Son so that human beings might see how divine love will save them. He does not send Jesus to condemn but rather to demonstrate that "God is love" and to show his true desire is to save the whole world.

Another way to express what I am saying is to see that God created us to *share* in a deep personal relationship, one that is the result of overflowing love. God is never distant from us, abiding in silence or rejection. He is near all of us (cf. Acts 17:22–28), giving each of us the opportunity to repent and trust him.

The late Baptist theologian Stanley Grenz (1950–2005) rightly said the statement "God is love is the very basis for understanding *all the so-called moral attributes of God*. Included in this divine love are such biblical ideas as grace, mercy and long-suffering patience; all of which speak of God's incredible goodness." Grenz concluded: "Because God is love, God is good—that is gracious, merciful, and long-suffering—in all he does. Above all, because God loves, he seeks the salvation and renewal of fallen creation."[14]

---

13. Swartley, *John*, 108.
14. Grenz, *Theology for the Community of God*, 95.

Chapter Four

Creation
The Gift of Love

> Rather than say that [God] created the universe out of nothing, we should say that he created the universe out of his own self, which is love.
>
> —METROPOLITAN KALLISTOS WARE

> To confess that God is the Creator is to say ... that the free, transcendent God is generous and welcoming.
>
> —DANIEL L. MIGLIORE

> The universe is the vineyard given to men by God. Everything is God's gift to man, a sign of his love.
>
> —DUMITRU STANILOAE

THE FIRST GOOD NEWS proclaimed in the Bible can be seen in the very first verse: "In the beginning God created the heavens and the earth" (Gen 1:1). *Creation is a majestic and gracious act of divine love. Our whole world is the gift of God's continuing love.* In creation we see that everything is God's gift to man, proving that we are active partners in a dialogue of eternal love. *Everything!*

Contrary to some popular thought, the world began in love and it will end in love. Jesus said that at the end of this age there will be "the renewal of all things" (Matt 19:28). This demonstrates that the same divine love that created the world will renew the world. *Christ's kingdom, begun on this earth, will be consecrated and completed on this same earth.* His kingdom is unconquerable but he never coerces. The more we offer the world back to God the more we confess that he really does "have the whole world in his hands."

Furthermore, the Genesis story shows that God did not create the universe out of nothing and leave. God created the universe by an act of his own free will.[1] He was not compelled to create by any force or power *outside* of himself. He freely chose to create. But why? "God's motive in creation is his love because God created the universe out of his own self, which is love."[2]

Creation is God calling "into existence the things that do not exist" (Rom 4:17). Think of it—the God who is love—who dwells in an eternal communion of love between the Father, Son and Holy Spirit—welcomes into existence a world of creatures different from himself. Here the crowning act of creation is clearly the human person made in God's own image and likeness. This reveals that God is much more than a master craftsman. He is a lover! "Creation is not so much of free will as of his *free love*."[3] Love desired a communion of persons, truly free beings who could share in God's eternal love in deep relationship.

How Should We Interpret Genesis 1–11?

Many Bible readers try to interpret the significant themes of Genesis 1–11—such as creation, the fall, the flood, and the Tower of Babel—as literal, historical events. (Huge divisions among conservative Christians are caused by debates over this argument.) I learned this literal reading of the story of creation and fall as a child. I preached it in my early years in ministry. I often had questions but I relied on my background to

---

1. St. Augustine said God did not create the universe out of preexisting matter. This means creation is a gift of God who was under no compulsion to create but this is not the only way faithful Christians have understood creation.

2. Ware, *Orthodox Way*, 44.

3. Ware, *Orthodox Way*, 44.

maintain this interpretation. Of course, none of the stories in the Genesis accounts are beyond God's power. But I now believe God's power is *not* the point in any of these vitally important stories. One conservative Old Testament scholar expresses how I hear these stories now: "However, important . . . the question of historicity may be, that is not central to these chapters; the main issue here is their theological significance."[4]

These early chapters of Genesis are concerned with what we call "pre-history." They deal with beginnings, e.g., the origin of the world and human failure. This leads us to the revelation of God's love. I now believe we can understand these chapters in a far better way than has generally been the case.

> [These chapters] continue to be divine revelation, but revelation given in a form that would make sense to those who received it, rather than necessarily appealing to modern standards of scientific and historical inquiry. Genesis 1–11 also describes the ever-deepening decline into sin, and so prepares us for the story of salvation, and the call of Abraham in Genesis 12.[5]

The Creation of the World in Love

From the beginning Jews and Christians have confessed that God is the creator of our world. In some sense the existence of our world is a divine act. This means that creation is a free act, not a necessary one. God was not driven to create by force or necessity. Thus, in creation there was no sense of compulsion in God. "Were God *driven* to create anything external to himself, this external reality would ultimately exercise sovereignty over the divine being."[6] In that case God would need the world to be who he is, thus he would not be eternal or transcendent. God remains who he is in himself *apart* from the world even though he is immanent in the world. But how can this be?

God's nature [which we've already seen is love] is already actualized apart from the world in the eternal relationship between the Father and the Son, which is the Holy Spirit.[7] God is God *without* the world. This means God creates the universe as an act of freedom. But why?

4. Routledge, *Old Testament Theology*, 130–31.
5. Routledge, *Old Testament Theology*, 131–32.
6. Grenz, *Theology for the Community of God*, 130.
7. Grenz, *Theology for the Community of God*, 130.

God *is* love within the eternal relationship of the Father, Son, and Spirit. Thus God is eternally self-giving. *The world flows out of eternal love.* "Precisely because creation is God's loving act, it is free, voluntary, and non-necessary."[8] This means God chooses to create the world in order to *share* love. But we should note that "the choice for creation is also a choice against the alternative, against the decision to not create."[9] Karl Barth rightly expressed this idea by saying that in creation God chooses "something" and rejects "nothing." God rejects the nothingness of the void by saying "no" to nonexistence.[10]

"Because God is love, God is self-giving. Because God is self-giving, God willingly creates the world."[11] Could it be that God creates us as partners for relationship? I believe so. God had choices about what kind of world to create and whether or not to even create it. Simply put, nothing in God's nature *required* him to create. God's passion in creation was to love and to be freely loved.

Is God Our Father?

We can now see that we are warranted to understand that God has a profoundly personal relationship with us and our world. The children's song says this well: "He's got the whole world in his hands." *In fact, the God who created the world is the father of all.* The late Scottish Reformed theologian T. F. Torrance clearly expressed this theology.

> A general conception of God as Father and Creator of all humankind was not wanting in the Old Testament. . . . [And] in the Gospels, as in the rest of the New Testament God is spoken of as "Father" in a two-fold way, in a *general way* as the Creator of mankind and the Provider for his human children, as "our Father who art in heaven" in the Lord's prayer, and in a *specific* way in his unique relational to the Son, as the God and Father of Jesus Christ (italics mine).[12]

In my background there was a profound reaction against God's universal fatherhood. Why? I think we feared that such an understanding

---

8. Grenz, *Theology for the Community of God*, 132.
9. Grenz, *Theology for the Community of God*, 132.
10. Barth, *Church Dogmatics* 3/I, 330–34.
11. Grenz, *Theology for the Community of God*, 133.
12. Torrance, *Christian Doctrine of God, One Being Three Persons*, 55–57.

might jeopardize the need for people to trust Christ for their salvation. But what if God is the Father of all human beings? What if everyone belongs to God in some basic sense? What if God loved us so much, and created us for his love, that he wants us to know him intimately as *our* Father? What if Jesus came to introduce us to our Father who already loves us? (I believe this is precisely what he did.) But when Jesus pointed out that a Syrian soldier and a gentile woman had more faith than anyone in their day, the hometown crowd tried to throw him off a cliff. In effect, Jesus said, "Your gospel is way too small." Jonathan Wilson-Hartgrove adds, "Better to celebrate that the scripture is fulfilled in our hearing than to grapple with the ways God's Word forces us to expand our imagination."[13]

Jesus came to villages preaching peace to all people. He preached "salvation to the ends of the earth" (cf. Isa 49:6). His peace was clearly intended for all people. But he met the most resistance from his own hometown. Jesus took this text from Isaiah about the great day of Jubilee and said it had arrived for everyone. When he pointed out that a Syrian soldier and a Gentile woman had more faith than anyone else in their day, the hometown crowd tried to throw him off a cliff. No one wants a prophet to speak so directly to them.

In the Old Testament we see that God was called "father" in the unique sense of relationship with Israel that we can see in the word "covenant." But God is also called "father" to all mankind because he created the world. Thus there is proper sense in which we can speak of God as the *Father of all people*. Several biblical texts clearly urge us to see this point (cf. Num 16:22; Eph 4:5–6; Heb 12:9; Acts 10:34–35).

Because God is the Creator who loves us, God is our Father. As created children, we should seek to know our Father and Creator. This pursuit should never end. In order to enter fully into Jesus' way of knowing the Father, John said: "This is eternal life, that they may know you, the only true God, and Jesus Christ, whom you have sent" (John 17:3). Jesus brings us into *intimate communion* with his Father.

When the apostle Paul appealed to the Athenians to trust in the risen Christ he began by saying that all people are his *offspring* (Acts 17:26–28).

> From one ancestor he made all peoples to inhabit the whole earth, and he allotted the times of their existence and the

---

13. Wilson-Hartgrove, "Everyone Belongs to God," 2.

boundaries of the places where they would live, so that they would search for God and perhaps fumble about for him and find him—though indeed he is not far from each one of us. For "In him we live and move and have our being"; as even some of your own poets have said,

"For we, too, are his offspring."

Paul's words are clear: God wants us to be close to God. However, he grants fatherly *closeness* to those who "search" and "fumble about for him" and "find him." (Ponder these words if you have trouble with my point here. When Paul began speaking to these non-Christian Greeks he was extremely generous.) It is well worth the effort to see that the God of creation seeks a close personal relationship with us as our Father. He does not hate us but rather loves us and seeks after us.

There is one other matter we should note in these texts. Paul said of God: "indeed he is not far from each one of us" (Acts 17:27). We should realize that God is always near us, never far away! And if he is near us then he is near us in love. Thus, "everyone who calls on the name of the Lord shall be saved" (Acts 2:21).

"Out of Nothing"

The ancient liturgy of John Chrysostom said, "Thou hast brought us into being out of nothing." What does "out of nothing" mean?[14] It is commonly agreed that these words mean God created the universe by an act of his will. This is transcendence. As we saw above God did not create out of *inner necessity*.

> God's motive in creation is his love. Rather than say that he created the universe out of nothing, we should say that he created out of his own self, which is love. We should think, not of God the Manufacturer or God the Craftsman, but of God the Lover. Creation is not so much an act of his free will [though as we've seen this is true] as of his *free love*. To love means to share... because he is a communion of persons [in the Trinity], who share in love with one another.... By voluntary choice God created the world in "ecstatic love," so that there might be

---

14. The Latin phrase for this is *creatio ex nihilo*, thus creation is out of nothing. The world is not part of God's being nor does anything coexist eternally with God (e.g., eternal unformed matter out of which the world is created). This idea stands in stark contrast to all forms of dualism and pantheism.

besides himself other beings to participate in the life and the love that are his.[15]

Divine love in creation is utterly astounding! But there is yet more to ponder about creation and love. "In God's heart and in his love, each of us has always existed. From all eternity God saw each of us as an idea or thought in his divine mind, and for each one from all eternity, he has a special and distinctive plan. We have always existed for him; creation signifies that at a certain point in time we begin to exist also for ourselves."[16] This means the world is not self-sufficient but *contingent* and *dependent*. We are never alone. We can never be ourselves *without* God. At every moment our very existence depends on nothing less than the love of God.

A Relationship or an Event?

In saying that the Creator is love we are not saying what many assume—that God set the world in motion at the beginning and everything now functions on its own. God is *not* the cosmic clockmaker. *Creation is continual. God remains deeply involved in all he made and preserves it for love.*

The Catholic theologian Louis Bouyer expressed the truth of God's continual involvement in creation well. "It follows reciprocally that creation cannot merely be reduced to the event that was the beginning of all things. It is a permanent situation in which the creature subsists at every instant, as well as at the first instant, and which makes it at all times the recipient of its being, a permanent gift of the Creator."[17]

In speaking and thinking of creation as continual we are warranted to say that creation is not so much an event as a *continuing relationship*. "If God did not continue to exert his creative will at every moment, the universe would immediately lapse into non-being; nothing could exist for a single second if God did not will it to be."[18]

In my evangelical background creation was not kept before our minds and hearts in worship. It became more of an argument against evolution and a way to explain how mankind sinned. The local church I am now a member of includes, in our Lord's Day liturgy, regular references to creation. (These refresh my deep response to the love and glory

---

15. Ware, *Orthodox Way*, 44.
16. Ware, *Orthodox Way*, 45.
17. Bouyer, *Dictionary of Theology*, 105.
18. Ware, *Orthodox Way*, 45.

of God as Creator.) Such words allow us to celebrate together the love of God in creation. Here, as one example, was a recent invocation in which we confessed what we've seen in this chapter.

> **Pastor:** In the name of the Father, and of the Son, and of the Holy Spirit. We come to worship in spirit and in truth.
>
> **Pastor:** If you ask the sky who God is,
>
> **Congregation:** the sky will tell you of God's reach.
>
> **Pastor:** If you ask the day who God is,
>
> **Congregation:** the sun will tell you of God's warmth.
>
> **Pastor:** If you ask the night who God is,
>
> **Congregation:** the moon will tell you of God's comfort.
>
> **Pastor:** "The heavens are telling the glory of God" (Ps 19:1). Are you listening?
>
> **Congregation:** We are listening! We will sing God's glory. Let us worship Holy God.

While we clearly see the love of God revealed in the New Testament, the doctrine was not invented by Christians. God's love was always present in the Old Testament. In the Psalms there are countless references to the *steadfast love* of the Lord. Psalm 136 mentions this steadfast love in all twenty-six verses. It would require an extensive treatment of scores of Old Testament texts to demonstrate my point but consider only a few, e.g. Genesis 31:10; 39:21; Exodus 34:6–7.

No One Falls Alone

The creation story in Genesis includes not only the pristine glory of divine creation but the sad story of human failure. This failure, commonly called "the fall," has consequences on a physical, moral, and spiritual level. Christians almost universally agree that this failure impacted the entire human race and the created world. But the Christian West and the Christian East do not understand our moral failure in precisely the same way. I have come to believe that this distinction can have an effect on how we actually hear the story of God as love. Let me explain.

In the West, the doctrine of the human fall was developed profoundly through the rigorous thought of St. Augustine (354–430). Augustine's view, which most English-speaking Christians learned from childhood, generally interpreted the fall in a juridical way. Augustine suggested that Adam's sin was passed on to us through sexual intercourse.[19] Thus we were "born in sin" and inherited Adam's rebellion as if we were there in Adam's choice to rebel. I confess I always had problems with this view since it seemed as if I was responsible for what I actually did not choose to do. In support of this view Romans 5:12–14 has been used as a proof-text; "sin came into the world through one man."

The Christian East never entirely accepted this interpretation. (I am persuaded that the earliest theologians, before Augustine, did not share this view either.) While both the East and the West take sin seriously, and both see the need for forgiveness and divine healing, "original sin" was clearly not understood in the same way. Metropolitan Kallistos Ware summarizes the position of the East.

> The doctrine of original sin means rather that we are born into an environment where it is easy to do evil and hard to do good; easy to hurt others, and hard to heal their wounds; easy to arouse men's suspicions, and hard to win their trust. It means that we are each of us conditioned by the solidarity of the human race in its accumulated wrong-doing and wrong-thinking, and hence well-being. And to this accumulation of wrong we have ourselves added by our own deliberate acts of sin. The gulf grows wider and wider.[20]

But do not all of us share in the fall of Adam? Should we all be punished because of his sin, Adam's sin, regardless of how we understand "original sin"? I am persuaded that we are all created in the image of God, thus we are both "independent and co-inherent."

> No man is an island. We are "members of one another" (Eph. 4:25), and so any action, performed by any member of the human race, inevitably affects all members of the human race. Even though we are not, in the strict sense, guilty of the sins of others, yet we are somehow always *involved*.[21]

---

19. In fairness, this does not mean sexual intercourse is itself evil.
20. Ware, *Orthodox Way*, 62.
21. Ware, *Orthodox Way*, 62.

Creation

How Do We Understand Sin?

It is helpful at this point to define sin. (Frankly, this is not easy to do.) Biblical scholars realize that no single English word can consistently translate one Hebrew word, or group of words. Thus, ideas like "a changed status" or "a rebellion against a superior" surface in attempts to translate the various words for "sin." Kenneth Grayson said the best thought might be "deviation from the right way." "Sin means the soul itself is diseased." Thus we can say, "The sinner contradicts the positive forces that uphold the community and have their root in God."[22] Thus sin is personal and communal. Far too many think of sin only as a private or personal flaw.[23]

Perhaps a straightforward definition of sin is needed at this point. The Greek word for sin means "to miss the mark." But what is the *mark that* we miss? Most of the teachers who influenced me said the "mark" was God's holiness; we miss this holiness by failing to live up to God's commands. Paul says "we all fall short of the glory of God" (Rom 3:23). But does missing God's glory simply mean to break God's commandments ? Yes and no. (Scripture does call us to be holy for sure; cf. 1 Pet 1:15–16). But how can we be holy? In Scripture to be 'holy' is not predominantly defined as following religious rules or laws. I would define holiness as "a way of maintaining peace and order within human institutions and relationships. Holiness is to have 'wholeness' in our lives and relationships."[24] The commands of God were not given to help us be like God. They were given to help us to be happy and healthy on God's earth. Remember, he called us to rule and to reign on his earth.

> Yet what is it that God desires? He desires that we live as emissaries, ambassadors, caretakers, and image-bearers on the earth. This means that humans become "holy" not by denying our role as humans on the earth, but by embracing it and living as much like human beings as we possibly can. God created us to be humans, and God wants us to be humans. Therefore, human holiness (and therefore a reflection of God's glory) is not accomplished through escaping the world, but by living as the images of God on earth, just as he created us.[25]

22. Richardson, ed., *Theological Word Book of the Bible*, 227–28.

23. How the church understood sin and the fall was widely and variously understood by the church fathers, something that should caution us against narrow definitions and dogmatic certainty.

24. Myers, *Nothing But the Blood of Jesus*, 43–44.

25. Myers, *Nothing But the Blood of Jesus*, 44.

We live best with one another and the earth when we keep God's laws. "Sin is not when we fail to live like God, but when we fail to live like humans. Sin does not just keep us from becoming godly; it keeps us from becoming human."[26] A number of modern biblical scholars have focused on sin in this way. Sin in all actions and attitudes leads us to harm both ourselves and others; sins such as rivalry, blame, scapegoating and violence. When this understanding is applied to New Testament texts we begin to see why and how Jesus came to save us from our sin, not simply to die so God could forgive our sins (cf. Matt 1:21).

Often fiction can capture the impact of the human fall into sin better than propositions. In the famous Russian novel *The Brothers Karamazov*, we hear Starets Zozima explain what the fall means when he says all are "responsible for everyone and everything." Here is an insightful dialogue in Dostoevsky's novel that clearly underscores this point.

> There is only one way to salvation, and that is to make yourself responsible for all men's sin. As soon as you make yourself responsible in all sincerity for everything and for everyone, you will see at once that this is really so, and that you are in fact to blame for everyone and for all things.[27]

The Tears of God

Over time I began to see how the doctrines of creation and fall point to great pain in God's heart. Let me explain. There are an abundance of biblical references to support the belief that God suffers. (Consider only three such texts: Judges 10:16; Jeremiah 31:20; and Hosea 11:8.) If any of these three passages means anything at all, they must mean that even before the incarnation God was directly involved in the sufferings of his creation. Our misery quite clearly causes grief to God; the tears of God are joined with those of man.[28]

Simply put, if God is love and God's love created the world then how could God remain *indifferent* to our sorrow and pain? If I told my son "I deeply love you" but I was indifferent to his pain and suffering, how would he know that I truly love him? God, our Creator, loves us and identifies with us in our anguish.

---

26. Myers, *Nothing But the Blood of Jesus*, 53.
27. Dostoevsky, cited by Ware, *Orthodox Way*, 62.
28. Ware, *Orthodox Way*, 63.

A Radical Understanding

The truth I am advocating here leads to a radically Christian understanding of love and life.

> In the immense cathedral which is the universe of God, each man, whether scholar or manual laborer, is called to act as the priest of his whole life—to take all that is human, and to turn it into an offering and a hymn of glory.[29]

> If a few men become prayer—prayer that is "pure" and to all appearances quite useless—they transform the universe by the sole fact of their presence, by their very existence.[30]

In my background I rarely celebrated God's creation as a magnificent work of divine love. In fact, I preached through Genesis but do not recall explaining *clearly* what God's love had to do with creation, much less how divine love appeared in God's response to our fall. The Creator made us for a face-to-face relationship that is not controlled. We are partners, no doubt junior partners, but partners nonetheless. But it took me some time to clearly see this truth too.

---

29. Paul Evdokimov, cited by Ware, *Orthodox Way*, 65.
30. Olivier Clément, cited by Ware, *Orthodox Way*, 66.

Chapter Five

Love Is Who God Is

> Love is the name most pleasing to God himself.
> —St. Gregory Nazianzus

> "God is love" takes us into the depths of the divine nature.
> —Rudolph Schnackenburg

> "God is love" is the best definition we can give of God, the most powerful thing we can say about him.
> —Metropolitan Hilarion Alfayev

In the 1990s I had the delight of visiting the beautiful country of Brazil. I preached at a conference in Rio. In the distance I could see the famous statue of Christ the Redeemer. It stands above the city on Mount Corcovado, a rocky peak in the Tijuca National Park in central Rio de Janeiro. The statue stands over a hundred feet high on its pedestal. Its expanded arms are over ninety feet wide.[1] This elevated Jesus is always visible. As we've

---

1. The original design was to place a globe in one of Christ's hands and a cross in the other. The idea seems to have been to show Christ's love for the whole world.

seen, the apostle John similarly elevated Christ above all other figures. For this, and a myriad of related reasons, no other person in human history has been written about more than Jesus of Nazareth. Think about that.

The popular evangelical writer Max Lucado, who once lived in Rio, refers to seeing the Christ the Redeemer statue daily. He says he often used it to guide him home when he became lost on the busy streets of this immense city. Lucado says: "John 3:16 offers you an identical promise. The verse elevates Christ to thin-air loftiness, crowning him with the most regal of titles: 'One and Only Son.'"[2]

Lucado is right—we must first look to Christ the Redeemer to find our way back home. He concludes: "Don't we need to learn? We know so much, and yet we know so little. The age of information is the age of confusion: much know-how, hardly any know-why. We need answers. Jesus offers them."[3]

We can truly find our way home by the light of the love of Christ.

But Is Love Who God Is?

It should be obvious by now: *the love of God is central to the Christian faith.* This is how we rightly understand God's nature. This truth gives us hope that God is not fickle, that he will receive us if we flee to him. This is why my first epigraph above cites St. Gregory of Nazianzus, called St. Gregory the Theologian, who said: "Love is the name most pleasing to God himself." Could this early church theologian be right?

I will say this more than once, because it is so important; we must continually resist prooftexting our ideas of God with Bible verses if we are to find our way to the biblical truth of God's love. We must begin by focusing our attention on *who God is*. This is why I am fully persuaded that if our doctrine of God is wrong almost everything else we believe will be wrong. Thus, to quote from biblical texts like we saw in chapter 3 is only a beginning. We must not just quote these verses and stop. And we most certainly should *not* do what I learned growing up—to pile up texts thinking this makes for a good argument. When we dig deep into the biblical narrative we soon discover that love is not something God does from time to time. *It is who God is all the time.* Put another way, love is not just a part of God, say one of his attributes among others. *Love is*

---

2. Lucado, *3:16*, 45
3. Lucado, *3:16*, 50.

at the center of God's being. Everything God is and does flows out of this inexhaustible love.

Søren Kierkegaard pondered the mysteries of Christ deeply when he wrote: "Oh, marvelous omnipotence of love! But God who creates out of nothing, who almighty takes from nothing and says, 'Be,' lovingly joins, 'Be something even in opposition to me.' Marvelous love, even his omnipotence is under the sway of love."[4] Consider—God's omnipotence is "under the sway of love." Abstract theological propositions can never reach such a marvelous conclusion.

When John says "God is love" (1 John 4:8) he is not speaking of the divinity in general. He has in mind God the Father "who sent his Son" (1 John 4:20) and who "has given us his Spirit" (1 John 4:13). "This aligns with the church's teaching that the Father is the *arche* or 'source' of the Godhead. . . . Love that is not shared is not love at all. A god who is a simple monad is neither person nor love."[5] The contemporary Orthodox theologian Vigen Guroian expresses this with incredible clarity: "God = Love. Love = God. In so much as human beings love, they grow into the likeness of God and they enter into communion with others."[6]

Had I picked up a book that made such claims forty years ago I would have reacted quite negatively. I argued then that the idea of God *being* love was reductionistic. Time has shown me how my thinking negatively impacted a great deal in my life and ministry. It has also shown me how some of my favorite teachers failed to see love as God's eternal being.

Thus my claim that God is love *cannot* be explored without taking into account the entire Bible. I believe that "The Old Testament notion of divine justice is complemented in the New Testament by the doctrine of God's love, which transcends justice. 'God is love' is the best definition we can give of God, the most truthful thing we can say about him."[7]

Earlier I said the love of God is central when we begin the human story with creation. Why? Creation is revealed as a *uniquely* divine act![8] German theologian Jürgen Moltmann rightly said the whole world was

---

4. *Bread and Wine*, 212.
5. Guroian, *Orthodox Reality*, 111.
6. Guroian, *Orthodox Reality*, 111
7. Alfayev, *Mystery of Faith*, 18.
8. When we get sidetracked in debates about the metaphors used in Genesis 1–2, and what part of the story is literal or not, we easily miss the central point—God is the Creator! He creates because of love, not to test or condemn. Even the judgment of Adam and Eve can be understood as an act of love.

created through a Trinitarian process whereby God works out of eternal love because love means self-communication of the good.[9] God is not the "Unmoved Mover" of Aquinas and Aristotle but the One who creates with deep self-involvement. I am taken back by Moltmann's claim that God's first act in creation was one of self-involvement and limitation. I happily resonate with this language now while acknowledging it can be misused. Moltmann traces the idea of love and creation through the witness of a large number of theologians down through the history of the church. This *limitation* is what he means by God's "self-humiliation." God creates because he loves and God loves so deeply that he gave up his only Son, who goes through humiliation and death to save us through his cross.

What I Missed in Theology

As I have already indicated my thesis equipped me to undertake some serious rethinking. If you skim this book you will likely miss my most important conclusions. I assure you that I did not discover that the love of God was essential to everything by searching popular theology books. Indeed, some of these books gave me an understanding that frankly starved my soul. These books answered the question of who God is by giving a list of divine attributes, e.g., sovereign, omnipotent, omniscient, omnipresent. Based on my personal observations you would certainly not know that God is love by listening to most sermons. Oh yes, love is sometimes mentioned, sometimes frequently. But divine love is almost never explored in terns of *who God is*. *God's love was rarely recognized as the central truth of Christian faith in my intellectual formation.*

"Smile, God Loves You"

To complicate matters the popular phrase "God loves you" can become remarkably trite! (We see smiley face stickers which say: "Smile, God Loves You.") We've actually created a context "[that] has been purged of anything culture finds uncomfortable. The love of God has been sanitized, democratized and above all sentimentalized."[10] I am persuaded that if we persist in thinking about God in such banal ways we will continue

---

9. Moltmann, *God in Creation*, 77.
10. Carson, *Difficult Doctrine of the Love of God*, 11.

to miss the robust truth of love. It might surprise you to know that we will spend all eternity exploring love. It behooves us to begin now.

In reaction to this trite approach I was once given a tract that said: "Mourn! God may hate you!" As bad as "Smile, God loves you" was, this line was a hundred times worse! G. K. Chesterton was right: "When a man ceases to believe in God, it is not so much that he believes in nothing, as it is that he is willing to believe in anything."[11] I believe this has happened to a great deal of American Christianity, causing it to end up in a desperate state. We have an *absent God*, thus there is a deep sense of darkness that pervades our lives. This absence is driving us to embrace extremes and ideologies that oppose the real truth of God's love. We watch cable television shows, listen to talk radio, and read inordinate amounts of opinion on social media. The results of this reality are destroying true spiritual life.

We Must Know God Beyond Our Words

What I missed in my education was what the late Romanian Orthodox theologian Dumitru Stăniloae called "the ever more sublime meaning of things, and of the words which express these things—even the words of Holy Scripture." To believe God is love should lead to a theology of God that does more than quote Bible verses. "We must rise beyond [these words] to the experience of the mystery of God and of his operations."[12]

Unless we rightly understand the centrality of this revealed mystery we will end up with a God who never judges and a love that is pure emotion. This is clearly not a robust view of the love of God who gave up his Son for the salvation of the world. If we do not explore what Wesley called God's "strange design," then I submit our worship will no longer be doxological. This will result in our thrashing about in a pool of religious narcissism!

The Awakening We Need

Many talk today about revival. I have serious doubts about most modern American claims for revival, especially given the fruit we see. Linking revival with Christian nationalism is a striking case in point. While I have no doubt that we need a true awakening, I would argue that this

---

11. Freeman, *Every Where Present*, 11.
12. Stăniloae, *Experience of God* 1, 106.

awakening must be rooted in *who God is!* We cannot assume Christians have a firm grasp on who God is when so much indicates the opposite. Previous American awakenings have often led us to enthusiasm and emotional passion, thus easily missing the central message of love. I am now convinced that the awakening we need must be rooted in a healthy understanding of God.[13]

Made for Freedom

Over time I have discovered how emotional and relational health come about through knowing and experiencing God's love. Until I reached my late thirties I privately wondered why so many intelligent and gifted Christians were so often unbalanced emotionally and relationally. I could see that many possessed a robust understanding of the Bible but their lack of compassion and kindness was alarming. Why? In grappling with this disconnect I came to understand what Christian psychiatrist George Benson meant when he said we need to *receive divine love in an undefended state*. He reasons that receiving unearned love is at the heart of both psychological and spiritual growth. This embrace of a proper understanding of divine love, and making it my deepest desire to experience it, will make a massive difference in real life.[14] This is the "freedom for which Christ has set us free" (Gal 5:1).

The late Swedish Lutheran theologian Nels F. S. Ferre expressed this idea of freedom well. He reasoned that God made us for fulfillment *through* freedom. In making us for himself, God created us for unconditional and universal love. We are thus free only as we find divine love from, for, in, and through God. The anxiety of the loveless is a chain of fear.[15]

---

13. Revival and awakening became a deep interest of mine as a young man. I experienced a move of the Spirit at Wheaton College in 1970 that accomplished a great deal of true good. But the more I wrote and studied this phenomena the more I questioned the long-term results of such movements. I actually wrote a book on revival in 1998, revised in 2001, titled *True Revival*.

14. Benson, *Silent Self*, 84.

15. Ferre, cited in White, *Eternal Quest*, 321.

"God Loves Me Immensely"

At the deepest level our lives are shaped by the people we know and the stories that transform us. In my life it has been through stories, from both the living and the dead, that my personal growth has taken shape.

Some years ago my understanding of God's love was profoundly reshaped by the story of an Italian Catholic named Chiara Lubich (1920–2008). Chiara was a young school teacher in the city of Trent during the Second World War. As bombs fell almost daily she formed a bond of love with several of her spiritual sisters. This bond of friendship led Chiara to devote her whole life to love. Upon first learning about Chiara, especially from those who personally knew her, I began to see how deeply she entered into divine love through the work of the Spirit. The beginnings of her spiritual journey were marked by a strong illumination that God is love. "The profound understanding of him that derived from this was for Chiara and for her companions to whom she immediately communicated her intuitions, an entirely new discovery. It was so dazzling as to lead them to a total change of mentality and of life."[16]

When Chiara was only twenty-three years old, living amidst daily death and dying, she *thirsted* for God. She desired to know how to fuel her ardent desire. She "saw with regret that the Christianity of her time too often appeared emptied of its vitality and its effectiveness."[17] Here is her description of what happened next.

> In the midst of all kinds of inconsistencies and contradictions, God was drawing me to himself. At a moment when the way we Christians were living deeply distressed me, he manifested himself.
>
> Exactly when, I do not know. His subtle light entered in and enlightened me. As it enwrapped my soul, it did not suppress my former ideas, but slowly replaced them with new ones.
>
> One fact I recall. I was still in school. A priest who was passing through . . . wanted to have a word with me. He asked me to offer up an hour of my day for his intentions. I answered: "Why not the entire day?" Struck by such youthful generosity . . . he told me: "Remember that God loves you immensely."
>
> *This was the blinding light* [italics added].
>
> "God loves me immensely." "God loves me immensely."

---

16. Cerini, *God Who Is Love in the Experience and Thought of Chiara Lubich*, 13.
17. Cerini, *God Who Is Love in the Experience and Thought of Chiara Lubich*, 13.

> I told it to my companions: "God loves you immensely, God loves you immensely."
>
> Since that moment I see God's presence everywhere with his love: in daytime, during the night, in my enthusiasm, in my resolutions, in events that are joyful and comforting, in situations that prove to be sad, awkward, or difficult.
>
> He is always there, he is present everywhere, and he explains things to me. What does he explain? *That everything is love.* All that I am and all that regards me. All that we are and all that regards us. That I am his child and he is my Father. That nothing escapes his love, not even the mistakes I make, because *he permits them*; that his love envelops Christians like myself, that it embraces the Church, the world, and the entire universe.
>
> And he sustains me and opens my eyes to see everything and everyone, especially so, as expressions of his love.
>
> The conversion has come about. The "novelty" has flashed through my mind: I know who God is. God is love.[18]

In Chiara's story you can see how God revealed himself to her as love. I began to see remarkable parallels in her story with the experience of so many other Christians, all from a myriad of backgrounds and traditions. This experience of God's love as immense became a major contribution to my growing ecumenical work among Christians of all traditions. I understood this was the experience of John and Charles Wesley as well as that of the Catholic mystic Julian of Norwich. The very popular modern Catholic writer Henri Nouwen had a similar story. (Personally, I think this is one reason why so many evangelicals have benefited from reading Nouwen.)

The language Chiara used is common to those who've encountered this divine love in the Spirit. She describes it as a mystical encounter with God, who is perfect, eternal, and inexhaustible love.

The Meaning of God-Love

As we've seen our words cannot *define* God. Further, the meaning of John's words—"God is love"—is not found in rationalistic arguments or emotional sentimentality. Nor can we use divine love to escape from experiencing suffering and pain. Divine love can reach us at the deepest level of our being. When it does it will project a human/divine sense of life through the words of Scripture. These words reveal to us the deep

---

18. Chiara's own words, as told by Cerini, *God Who Is Love in the Experience and Thought of Chiara Lubich*, 13–14.

sense that God is *eternally* love. Perhaps we get so little from our Bible reading because we miss this central truth.

Notice what Chiara is *not* saying: "love is God." This statement is not *entirely* wrong but it can easily project a human notion of love *being* God. This is never *precisely* true. This borders on pantheism. Real evil does exist and it truly opposes love. But evil is not equal with God in any meaningful sense. Thus Christians must not embrace what is called dualism.[19]

When I first began to understand Chiara's use of the hyphenated expression God-Love I realized more clearly than ever that true Christianity must begin with God. When I shared this discovery with my friend, the late Fr. Thomas Baima, a wonderful relational oneness began between us; me an evangelical Protestant and Tom a Roman Catholic priest and theologian. Tom became my closest partner in ecumenism and was a confidant in my own spiritual direction. When he heard me speak about Chiara's idea of God-Love he asked if I knew where she got this description. He had discovered the same idea in Catherine de Hueck Doherty (1896–1985). Doherty, originally an Orthodox Christian, was born into a wealthy Russian family that escaped to Canada during the Russian Revolution. She eventually became a Catholic lay apostle, social activist, and pioneer in the struggle for interracial justice. Catherine was a wonderful spiritual writer, lecturer, and "mother" to both priests and laity. She became a close collaborator with well known influencers like Thomas Merton, Peter Maurin, and Dorothy Day. (She exchanged significant letters with Merton that you can find in his published letters.) Tom told me Catherine used this same expression as Chiara: God-Love.[20] *She wanted to show how Christianity begins in God's heart, not in the Creed.* "The Divine nature is love. Love is not something that comes from God. Love is God and God is love. If a Christian were to name the Divine in English, the best term would simply be 'God-Love.'"[21] I have come to agree that this lovely English shorthand for "God is love" keeps this truth before us in a unique way.

---

19. Dualism is the idea that all of life is separated into two main categories: the secular and the sacred. This is a fragmented vision of reality that puts "spiritual" things in the "sacred" category and "worldly" things in the "secular" category. Dualism also creates a conflict between God and evil in which these are two *supreme forces* that govern our universe, good and evil.

20. Neither I nor Fr. Tom could determine who used this hyphenated word first. But we marveled that two different lay women, whose lives overlapped to a large extent, had given us the best simple description we have of the nature of God.

21. Baima, "Christianity: Origins and Beliefs."

God-Love is alone eternal and always remains so because it is the reality of who God is in his eternal being. God-Love avoids the dangers of pantheism, the idea that God is everything. It also avoids deism, the notion that the transcendent God is not personally involved in our lives. Christianity is emphatically clear about this—God is not to be overly *identified* with the world, which is God's creation. God is everywhere present, thus immanent. But he is not "in" everything, as pantheism teaches.

Second, we can say that the Christian life is *a continual progress into the full revelation* of God-Love. We face moral ambiguities and perplexing questions. But the way forward is always to remind ourselves that the deepest resources of God-Love are unfolding in and through us. As Chiara's story shows, *we do not need to become academic theologians to live this way.* I am persuaded we need, more than ever, a working theology of God-Love. Perhaps, by using this hyphenated description for God we can more consistently associate love with God's very being.[22]

God Really Does Love You

As a college student in the sixties I shared my faith using a popular booklet that began with the well-known sentence: "God loves you and has a wonderful plan for your life." Though such a simple statement can be easily misunderstood, as noted above, I now see the truth of this (so-called) "first spiritual law." I believe Augustine envisioned this in his *Confessions.* The Quaker William Penn said the same thing when he reasoned that if we grasp God's love we shall all be lovely, and in love with God and one another.

The Anglican priest William Law (1686–1761) wrote a great deal about holy living. Several of his books profoundly shaped the eighteenth century evangelical revival in Great Britain, especially through John and Charles Wesley and George Whitefield. He said *the greatest idea we can ever frame about God is to conceive of him as infinite love and perfect goodness.*

Amen.

---

22. The Orthodox monk Lev Gillet used another term, "Lord-love," to describe God.

Chapter Six

Can God's Love Be Defined?

In the Scripture the love of God is "intimately personal."
—Jordan Wessling

Lord, you have come to us as a small child, but you have brought us the greatest of all gifts, the gift of eternal love.
—St. Bernard of Clairvaux

I am not a smart man but I know what love is.
—Forrest Gump

WHEN YOU CAREFULLY READ the New Testament you will soon see that the Christian gospel consistently points us to God's love as the basis for everything good in our world. This truth runs like a thread through the entire story of Jesus and the apostles. For that matter love is a prominent theme in the Old Testament, though it clearly is not as openly stated as in the New. God pours out his love upon all his children because he is gracious. Love leads to an abundant expression of God's grace in divine mercy.

The late Old Testament scholar Terrence C. Fretheim suggested that Israel's understanding of the God-world relationship lies between two images, that of the monarchical and the organismic. By the first he means that God stands above and beyond the world. This can be seen in words such as "sovereignty" and "freedom." But the organismic image is equally important and has often been missed. This image reveals God's desire for *intimacy* with Abraham, Moses, Israel, and ultimately the whole world. This can be seen in many texts in "a relationship of reciprocity." This idea reveals how relationship defines our experience of God. "God is the transcendent Lord; but God is transcendent not in isolation from the world, but in relationship to the world."[1]

In the New Testament divine love is consistently *modeled on the selfless sacrificial love of Jesus* (John 13:34; 1 Cor 12:31; 13:1; 1 John 2:7; 4:10). Thus Jesus lived, died, and rose again for us and for our salvation out of love. "The Christian gospel testifies to the God of love who is not content to keep that love to Himself but instead lavishes it upon His children. . . . Here we see a love that values humans, in that God deems it worthwhile to perform such extraordinary actions for them."[2]

God *Proved* His Love

I can remember when I first heard the idiom "talk is cheap." It meant something like this: words are never enough, action is required. This idiom is a stark reminder that promises without action hold little value.

The apostle Paul writes in a way that demands action, especially when he speaks of the experience of those who know God in Christ. He says: "God's love has been poured into our hearts through the Holy Spirit that has been given to us" (Rom 5:5). He adds: "But God proves his love for us in that while we still were sinners Christ died for us" (Rom 5:8). Later Paul says: "Who will separate us from the love of Christ" (Rom 8:35)? The apostle clearly believed that the love of God gives us strength for life and hope for tomorrow. He also believed divine love will bring radical change.

But how do we *understand* this divine love?

---

1. Fretheim, *Suffering of God*, 35.
2. Wessling, *Love Divine,* 39. Much in this chapter is based on the seminal insights of theologian Jordan Wessling.

A Reasonable Way

Most definitions of love include the idea of benevolence. But benevolence explains, at a bare minimum, that it was for kindness and goodness that Christ died for us. I submit that benevolence is right but it does *not* go far enough. Why? In Scripture the love of God is "*intimately personal as well.*"[3]

The argument I wish to advance says the central insight of Christianity is to communicate the unfathomable love of God. Divine love creates, nurtures, and perfects the universe. It is action, not mere talk. The transforming fire of love, fully revealed in Jesus Christ, invites us to share in the life of the Trinity as God-Love. Thus the question we should ultimately ask is this: What will you *do* with infinite, eternal God-Love? I am persuaded there is only one way to discover the true nature of Christianity. By faith we must live in God-Love and commit ourselves to a truly radical way of life. Only then will we begin to experience for ourselves that God is love.

We have already seen that God loves the whole world. The Fourth Gospel provides even more than a few hints that God-Love is far more than benevolence. John 17 reveals that the love between the Father and the Son is a *shared communion that promotes unity*. John says God desires to share *his love* with humanity (cf. John 17:1–10; 15:1–11; 17:20–26; 1 John 4:4–21). Thus the love Jesus shares with us is the love of the Father *for* the Son, and of the Son *for* his Father. Add to these texts the truth of God's design for our deification (2 Pet. 1:4; John 17:24) and you get a clear idea of how divine love *transforms*. But this is not all. We see Christ's preparation of the church to be his holy bride (Eph 5:25–27), as well as Jesus' calling of his own disciples to be his "friends" (John 15:15). Both of these ideas help us embrace a much deeper understanding of love. These, and many similar texts, clearly show us that God's love is a "kind of intimate relational or interpersonal component alongside benevolence."[4]

So what does this mean for defining God-Love? An appreciation for seminal biblical texts will allow us to see that God-Love *includes God's desire for our intimate union with him*. The challenge is to make sense of these Scriptures and then to see how they can be integrated into a theologically fruitful conception of love. Jordan Wessling has provided a

---

3. Wessling, *Love Divine*, 39. Italics are mine.
4. Wessling, *Love Divine*, 39–40.

model for properly defining God's love that he calls "the Value Account of God's Love."

Embracing the Value Account of Love

Wessling's "value account" of love has given me a much deeper understanding of divine love.[5] By going beyond God's benevolence and desire for union with us we can better understand why we are directed to love with *imitative love*. Imitative love should be directed to God, to others, and even to ourselves (cf. John 15:9–17; 1 John 4:7–12; Matt 5:43–48; Eph 5:1–2). Thus we are warranted to center the origin of God's love within the intra-trinitarian life of the Father, Son, and Holy Spirit, a love that existed "before the foundation of the world" (John 17:24).

If the New Testament warrants belief in this understanding of love then it is helpful to conclude that there are five *manifestations* of love: (1) God's intra-Trinitarian love; (2) God's love of humans; (3) the human love of God; (4) the human's love of another person; and (5) the human's love of self. After a lifetime of reading and studying these biblical texts I believe Jordan Wessling's value account is both satisfying and immensely helpful.[6]

The value account also warrants us to see divine love as *God's desire for the beloved's good*. "In fact, it is difficult to find a Christian account of love that does not see desiring and/or willing the beloved's good as essential to love."[7] Read this sentence several times and you may begin to see the significance of this way of defining God's love.

This value account works in several important ways. First, it provides a clear explanation of what it means to *genuinely* value another. Simply put, this "postulates that God loves humans in a deep, dignity-affirming way."[8] But it does not mean that God loves us more than he loves himself. Wessling is surely correct: "[T]he cross reveals that God loves humans as worth dying for; it would be perverse, on the present value account, to suppose that God loves anything as much as or more than He who is the fount of all truth, beauty, and goodness."[9]

---

5. The "value account" is an idea rooted in analytical philosophy that Jordan Wessling employs to explain how we can better understand the meaning of divine love.

6. Wessling, *Love Divine*, 43–44.

7. Wessling, *Love Divine*, 57.

8. Wessling, *Love Divine*, 72.

9. Wessling, *Love Divine*, 73.

Several truths stand out when the value account is adopted:

1. The valuing of the existence of the one loved.
2. The valuing and flourishing of the one loved.
3. The valuing of the union of the one loved in a multifaceted form of friendship.

Now, we can better answer the question—"What is divine love?" The value account gives several reasonable insights that help us to understand how God's love changes us, allowing us to love others as Jesus commanded (cf. 1 John 4:19).

Why Do Some Reject Such an Account?

One of the most influential books on divine love in the twentieth century was Anders Nygren's *Agape and Eros: The Christian Idea of Love*. The influence of this one book, especially on a number of Protestant ministers in the twentieth century, remains strong among those who have not even read Nygren's thought. In his view *agape* is, strictly speaking, only "gift-love." God's love does not find a person worthy of love but rather God's love causes a person to *become* worthy by virtue of God's gift. Nygren concludes that humans have *no intrinsic worth until God makes them valuable*.

There are two major flaws in this understanding. First, it is rooted in misunderstanding the way several Greek words are used for love. As a result this understanding becomes *arbitrary*. Second, it bestows value only after it *gives* love, thus we are said to be *intrinsically* valueless. My problem with this is simple. *If Jesus died for us on the cross we cannot be valueless beings.* Theologian Eleanor Stump rightly says divine love must include at least two desires: (1) The desire for the well-being of the one loved; and, (2) The desire to be united with the one loved.[10] But still we must ask *why*. It seems clear that God has good reasons to love us. He created us, he provides for us what we need, and he grants us the desire to know him. In fact, from creation God has always valued us!

One of the most common objections to this account is that God's primary acts in creation and providence are for "his own glory." This idea, sometimes called "glorificationism," was powerfully made by Jonathan Edwards. It still influences a great deal of modern evangelical theology.

---

10. Stump's thought about how love values us is developed in Wessling, *Love Divine*, 53–69 and 66–68.

I once embraced it myself. Yet, even though the Scripture says a great deal about God's glory it never *explicitly* says this is *the singular reason* why God created us and cares deeply for the world. Ironically God's glory cannot be the reason he creates because "all glory" belonged to God long *before* he made the universe. And nothing can *increase* God's glory!

In philosophy of religion there is a category called "the general problem of creation." This quest takes us back to the statement I made earlier about God as a rational Being.[11] *If God creates for a particular reason (love) then that reason informs all subsequent actions of God.* As we've seen, both creation and divine providence show us that God creates and sustains us out of love.

Our North Star

I do not propose to solve all of the problems we face in trying to understand divine love. Rather, I aim at a demonstration of *how* "God is love" makes the entire biblical story life-changing. In my experience divine love has allowed me to read the Scripture with a theological North Star! I concur with John Wesley, who in a sermon on 1 John 4:16 said, "Love is God's reigning attribute."[12] Can we not at the least agree on this? Love reigns! A popular song sung in many churches today is titled: "Our God Reigns." I love this title but the words reveal the problem with this kind of theology. Why? God does reign but the *reason* is because of who God is—God-Love!

I hope you can now see that my conclusion is not about embracing a *particular system* of theology. Protestants often disagree about doctrines like election and foreknowledge. I am persuaded that there must be room to disagree on these doctrines and remain faithful to orthodox theology. Writers and theologians in the Eastern and Western Church affirm divine love, even though in different ways. So, as we go further along, please keep in mind that the incarnation of Jesus changed the whole world whether people see it or not! We are, as J. B. Phillips put it, "The visited planet."[13]

---

11. God is sensible, reasonable, and has sound reasons for what he does. He cares for creation for a reason. But he cannot be *understood* through rational means. It is important to add that God's truth is *never* irrational but rather is truth that transcends rationality.

12. Wesley's "Notes" are available online from various sources. I consulted the Wesley Center Online at www.wesley.nnu.edu.

13. Phillips, *New Testament Christianity*, 92–93.

Hans Urs Von Balthasar was one of the most widely respected Roman Catholic theologians in the twentieth century. (Balthasar was much loved by Pope Benedict XVI.) In his written work Balthasar rigorously analyzed what he called *the nature of God's love*. He outlined two interpretative frameworks that Christians have traditionally used. The first framework Balthasar called *the cosmological system*. This system can be seen in the first stages of early Christianity. The second stage he called *the anthropological reduction*. This framework was developed after the Renaissance. Balthasar found both of these ideas wanting. Why? *They interpret God's actions from man's point of view*. He believed there was wisdom in both approaches but concluded they can only offer us a *relative* wisdom. He believed that what was ultimately viable was "the authentic center and motive of revelation, the boundless love of God." Simply put, Balthasar brought his readers back to God-Love as the Christian North Star for theology. His words, "the boundless love of God," underscore my entire thesis quite beautifully.[14] He treats love as *self-surrender* because, he rightly says, the very essence of God is self-surrender. But why? God values what he loves.[15]

Love Is Not an "Easy" Doctrine

Saying God's love is boundless does not mean it is ever *easy* to understand, a mistake often made by those who try to center their theology in divine love. This is true for many reasons, some of which we've already seen. (The title of D. A. Carson's book, *The Difficult Doctrine of the Love of God*, expresses precisely what I mean here.) The word *difficult is* an appropriate recognition of this problem. In my days as a pastor I think I first considered the subject of divine love to be *difficult* when I heard Dr. Carson address it in a ministerial fellowship I led. Without having previously thought deeply enough about this, I found myself saying that he has to be right about this word "difficult" with regard to God's love.[16]

---

14. Balthasar, *Love Alone is Credible*, from the book's back cover and preface.
15. Clements, *Meaning of the World is Love*, 43.
16. While Dr. Carson helped me dive into this difficult subject with new openness, I soon discovered a comprehensive witness to divine love in the larger church which helped me swim into these waters beyond the confines of my previous perspective.

Two Evangelical Authors on Divine Love

J. I. Packer (1926–2020) and A. W. Tozer (1897–1963) are two evangelical authors who have helped multitudes of Christians embrace a better understanding of God. (To be entirely forthright, Jim Packer was my very good friend for decades. I only knew Tozer from afar by talking to several friends who knew him personally.) I have undying admiration for both these men. Their life and work have given untold blessings to me.

When I preached on the nature of God over forty years ago I found two classic books the most helpful in my study. One was Packer's *Knowing God* (over one million copies sold). The other was Tozer's *The Knowledge of the Holy* (over two million copies sold). Both were immensely indispensable aids to my reading. Packer's chapter twelve, "The Love of God," was one of the best short treatments of God's love I had read, at least up to that point in my life. He begins by saying that John's three texts, which say that God is love, give us "one of the most tremendous utterances in the Bible—and also one of the most misunderstood. False ideas have grown up around it like a hedge of thorns, hiding its real meaning from view . . . ."[17] Like so many writers Jim Packer was concerned to protect the truth of divine love from the massive errors about God's nature that he saw in the church. When Packer defines love he calls it "a spontaneous determination of God's whole being in an attitude of benevolence and benefaction, an attitude freely chosen and firmly fixed."[18] Note that Packer uses the words "benevolence and benefaction" to describe love. This is the view which I now believe does not go nearly far enough in explaining the full meaning of love as deeply valuing us.

Packer's theological views are crystal clear: "God loves all in some ways" so that "everyone whom he creates, sinners though they are, receives many undeserved gifts in daily providence," and he "loves some in all ways" in that "in addition to these gifts of daily providence he brings them to faith, to new life, and to glory according to his predestinating purpose."[19] On this view God loves all persons in some respects but he loves only some fully for they alone will receive the benefits of eternal life. What I find surprising, the longer I have pondered Packer's view of God's love, is how so many who reject Packer's Puritan theology of

---

17. Packer, *Knowing God*, 17.
18. Packer, *Knowing God*, 121.
19. Packer, *Knowing God*, 124–26, gives a summary of what I conclude here.

predestination and election endorse these ideas about God. Perhaps this says more about Jim's irenic spirit and clear voice than anything else.

A. W. Tozer, on the other hand, is a bit less clear about the meaning of divine love, which he addresses in Chapter 20: "The Love of God." While Tozer does not articulate a discernible theological system about God and election, at least as clearly as Packer does, he begins his chapter by saying:

> The apostle John, by the Spirit, wrote, "God is love," and *some have taken his words to be a definitive statement concerning the essential nature of God. This is a great error.* John was by those words stating a fact, but he was not offering a definition.
>
> *Equating love with God is a major mistake* which has produced much unsound religious philosophy and has brought forth a spate of vaporous poetry completely out of accord with the Holy Scriptures and *altogether of another climate from that of historic Christianity.*
>
> Had the apostle declared that love is what God is, we would be forced to infer that God is what love is. If literally God is love, then literally love is God, and we are all duty bound to worship love as the only God there is [italics all mine].[20]

There is much in Tozer's chapter to commend. For example, he says, "For our souls' sake we must learn to understand the Scriptures. We must escape the slavery of words and give loyal adherence to the meanings instead."[21] I could not agree more. In fact, this is what I argued in rejecting prooftexting about the nature of God. Nevertheless I find Tozer's chapter on divine love one of the most unsettling things I read during my early formative period. For a man known as a so-called "evangelical mystic" I find it disconcerting that Tozer missed the great truth of God-Love by reacting against what one calls "spineless" love. Tozer knew the thoughts of certain mystics quite well, which makes this conclusion even more disappointing. He seems oblivious to the theology of divine love seen in an important mystic such as Julian of Norwich, who wrote so wonderfully about God's love. He also seems completely unaware of the fathers of the Eastern church, at least on this subject.

---

20. Tozer, *Knowledge of the Holy*, 151–52.
21. Tozer, *Knowledge of the Holy*, 152.

The Truth of Divine Transcendence[22]

There should be no doubt in our minds that the Bible reveals God as transcendent; i.e., beyond human understanding. In Scripture God's nature and power are wholly independent of the material universe, thus beyond all physical laws. But the Bible just as clearly reveals how the word "absolute" is not the best way to understand God's being. If the word "absolute" is coupled with transcendence we quickly end up with a god in isolation, or in a god of non-relatedness. When this happens the Bible's own story is lost.

The idea of transcendence is rightly used to safeguard God's being from dependence on human persons. *Thus this is an important truth.* Clearly, God does not *need* us. But this is where the truth of God's love should lead us to recognize that he could never be *indifferent* to the world. In fact God is personally related to our world in the closest possible way. "Clarity is not served by starting with an idea or thing-like substance or principle of which one predicates such impersonal attributes as infinite, eternal, immutable, absolute, and then continuing by adding on such personal attributes as loving, merciful and just."[23] This type of theology is what kept me from God's love.

Where Then Is God?

Properly understood, the word "transcendence" introduces us to the most bewildering questions we face in trying to understand God-Love: "Who is, and where is, God?"

I am old enough to remember when the Soviet cosmonaut Yuri Gagarin returned from the first space flight around the world. He said that he did not see God. The response of Christians was to generally make humor about his claim. For Christians, Gagarin's comments simply proved that God is a nonmaterial being. My point is this—Christians would never conceive of God as physical or quasi-physical. This is part of what John meant when he wrote "God is spirit and those who worship him must worship in spirit and truth." (John 4:24).[24] But is this all he meant?

---

22. I use the word "transcendence" throughout this book to mean "existing apart from and not subject to the limitations of the material universe."

23. Shaw, *Who Is God?*, 69.

24. Brown, *Gospel of John*, 180. Brown says the flesh and spirit contrast is not saying God is immaterial but rather there is a contract between flesh and spirit as "below" and

If God is *not* a material or physical object, where then is God located? Many believers retain the odd notion that God lives in some physical place. Many even refer to God as "the Man Upstairs." When surveyed most Americans say God lives "up in heaven." In my childhood background this is how I thought. *But this idea promotes isolation.* If we have enough faith, or the right kind of faith, we will go to heaven when we die (we thought in terms of heaven as a place up above). In this popular view God easily became alienated from our sinful world. I was taught to believe that Jesus would come again to destroy our messed-up planet. This coming again would happen after Christ had taken faithful Christians away in what one teacher called "the Great Snatch."[25] Christ would establish a thousand-year reign on the earth and then come again (for a second time) to judge and burn up the world in a great conflagration of total destruction. But nothing could be further from the truth taught in Scripture.

The central affirmations of the Bible give us an entirely different picture. The creed says nothing of this now-popular idea. You will not find it in the church for over 1,800 years. As we have already seen, God spoke with Moses as a person speaks with another person. In other Old Testament accounts we see God "meet" with certain persons, often by fire as in the case of Moses and the burning bush. But Christians universally confess that God finally revealed himself in the coming of Jesus the Logos, the eternal Word of God. *In Jesus the gospel of the kingdom transforms lives and brings God's reign into the present age.* God-Love is thus made known in ways that frame our entire life. And this kingdom will come in final fullness and power at the end of this present age.

God Restoring Creation

The Scriptures tell us that Jesus will complete what he began. He will reconcile the whole world to his Father. How can I say this? "For in him all the fullness of God was pleased to dwell, and through him God was pleased to reconcile to himself all things, whether on earth or in heaven,

---

"Spirit and truth" as above. Jesus' statement has nothing to do with a contrast between external and internal worship. This saying is shifting the emphasis in worship away from a one place or another, e.g., Mt. Gerizim or Jerusalem. The idea of purely internal worship actually denies the place for eucharistic gatherings, singing, praying together, baptism in water, etc.

25. This idea is also called "the rapture." The person I heard use this phrase was the popular author Hal Lindsey.

by making peace through the blood of his cross" (Col 1:19–20). Acts 3:21 refers to this as the time of "universal restoration" (*apokatastasis*). God's love will *not* be frustrated by sin. Christ will reign in grace.

The Christian tradition has always understood the story of Moses' encounter with the burning bush as an encounter with the flame of God-Love in restoring grace. What we are warranted to ask then is this: How does this fire of love draw the whole universe into the Trinity? The light that shines around the saints is never a cool, gentle light.[26] It is the blazing light of the consuming fire that Christ came to cast upon the earth (Luke 12:49). "It is the 'living flame of love,'" St. John of the Cross experienced. It burns and transforms all those it touches."[27]

---

26. If you've looked at Christian icons you know that fire/light is often the background to the person represented.

27. Zaleski, *Who Is God?*, 122.

Chapter Seven

Does Love Suffer?

> There is a sense in which God can be said to bear our sorrows.
> —J. K. Mozley

> The belief that God is a suffering God has become compelling for recent theology.
> —Paul Fiddes

> God is not a suffering at a distance God; God enters into the suffering of all creatures and experiences their life.
> —Terence E. Fretheim

JUST BENEATH THE SURFACE of what we've seen to this point we begin to understand that the usefulness of theological terms is abstract unless we give concrete meaning to the words we use when we speak of God. The twentieth century Dutch Reformed theologian Hendrikus Berkhof (1914–1995) understood this as well as any modern Protestant theologian. He said we must "dare to speak of not just . . . God's being but his 'character,' and with that about what is the heart of the Christian faith. We do this by stating first of all that the high and holy God in coming to us [and] manifests himself as Love."[1]

When I initially began to rethink my long-held views about the nature of God I encountered several problematic ideas that theologians generally have that are related to what is called *divine impassibility*. The central question is this: Does God *experience* pain and suffering with those he loves? Put another way: Does God have emotions? Classical theism says the answer is no. I began to doubt this "no" answer the more I wrestled with Scripture.

Augustine, for example, said God did not truly grieve over the suffering of the world. Anselm said God did not experience compassion. John Calvin said when the Scripture speaks of God's compassion, it employs a figure of speech that is an accommodation to our finite understanding. This is the way I learned the doctrine of God and explained the "divine attributes." Reformed theologian Daniel Migliore expresses this view well.

> Even the gospel witness to the suffering Christ on the cross was not able to dislodge the ancient philosophical presuppositions of divine immutability and impassibility from theological reflection. Numerous theologians, including Calvin, attempted to reconcile God's presence in Christ with the conviction that God does not suffer. Looking for support in classical two-natures Christology, they affirmed that while the human nature of Jesus suffered, the divine nature remained impassible.[2]

It must be noted that this idea was largely influenced by a type of Greek thinking that posited that a perfect God *was incapable* of suffering. Why? Suffering means there is change and God is an *unchanging perfect being*. Thus the idea of impassibility arose in early Christian thought. It remains influential in large portions of the church.

Following the greatest Greek philosophers—Aristotle, the Stoics and even the Epicureans—it was argued that "God was without passions." Tertullian even said, "The Father is incapable of suffering in company with another." Centuries later Anselm wrote: "Without doubt the divine nature is impassible." Thomas Aquinas said God cannot "repent, nor be

---

1. Berkhof, *Christian Faith*, 118.
2. Migliore, *Faith Seeking Understanding*, 85.

angry or sorrowful, since all these denote passion and defect."[3] (Note the consistent proximity of emotion with defect.)[4]

Shortly after the Protestant Reformation the idea of divine impassibility was confessed in catechisms and confessions. *The Westminster Confession* (1647), to cite one example, states: "There is but one living and true God, infinite in being and perfection, a most pure Spirit, invisible, without body, parts, or *passions*" (Chapter 2:1). This idea about *passions* prevailed in much of Reformation Protestantism until the twentieth century. Many modern theologians now question it.[5] I think these questions are being raised for good reason.

Resisting Speculative Ideas

If God is love and God is eternal then it seems clear that before anything else was, God was always love. But is God emotional or nonemotional? Is God impassible (imperturbable) as some argue? Further, did Jesus show real emotion? Did his love include desire, enjoyment, or both? And, is God's love unconditional or conditional? Frankly, what on earth do these terms actually mean?

The view of divine love I was taught by evangelical scholars followed the dominant conceptions of divine love taught by classical theism throughout the ages. Although classic theism is not monolithic, it generally refers to the conception of God as necessary and self-sufficient, perfect, simple, timeless, immutable, impassible, omniscient, and omnipotent.[6] The conclusion the great Augustine reached is, to my present understanding, quite astounding.

> In what way then does [God] love us? As objects of use or as objects of enjoyment? If He enjoys us, He must be in need of good from us, and no sane man will say that; for all the good we enjoy is either Himself, or what comes from Himself. . . . He does not

---

3. All cited in Thiselton, *Thiselton Companion to Christian Theology*, 481.

4. This approach obviously required a specific interpretation of scores of texts about God feeling and loving in the Old Testament. The finest biblical treatment on this I've found is *The Suffering of God*, by Terence E. Fretheim.

5. Some have argued that this questioning is the result of liberalism in theology. I believe this direction is because of a desire to do biblical theology *without* employing Greek categories for divine perfection.

6. Peckham, *Love of God*, 17.

enjoy us then, but makes use of us. For if He neither enjoys nor uses us, I am at a loss to discover in what way He can love us.[7]

I find this astounding. Read it again, even more carefully. God's love is not acquisitive. God gains no value or enjoyment from the world since he lacks nothing, an idea that has been called aseity. Divine love is only beneficence. Here is Augustine's point—divine love excludes a freely reciprocal love relationship between God and human persons.

This Western classical view was further developed by Thomas Aquinas, who said God loves universally but he does not love all equally. He wills "all some good; but He does not wish every good to them all," and so as far as "He does not wish this particular good—namely, eternal life—He is said to hate or reprobate them."[8] The idea of reprobation clearly predates Reformation theology but many Reformers continued to boldly teach it.

For Martin Luther love was similarly unilateral, unmotivated, and wholly gratuitous beneficence akin to grace. God is the giver who never receives. "God does not love because of our works: He loves because of His love."[9] While I agree that God loves because he loves I do not agree that his love is *only* beneficence. Luther, reacting against Augustine's understanding of human love (*caritas*), understood the love of God as the cause of all authentic love. Peckham is right: "Whereas Luther breaks significantly from Augustine and Aquinas regarding the value of human love, Luther's view of God's love is generally congruous with both."[10]

The modern scholar Carl F. H. Henry, called by *Time* magazine "the leading theologian of the nation's evangelical flank," insisted that "God is not a vague universal cosmic love but [rather] is wrathful toward fallen humanity and needs to be placated." Henry, like most of the evangelicals who influenced me, conjectured that an emphasis on divine love might easily eclipse divine holiness, justice, and judgment. He was concerned to "preclude any promotion of love at the expense of righteousness."[11] This perspective is much like that of Packer and Tozer that we previously saw. These strong warnings about how to not misunderstand the meaning of

---

7. *On Christian Doctrine*, cited in Peckham, *Love of God*, 18.
8. *Summa Theologica*, cited in Peckham, *Love of God*, 19.
9. Luther, *Works* 31; 57, cited by Peckham, *Love of God*, 20.
10. Peckham, *Love of God*, 21.
11. Henry, cited by Peckham, *Love of God*, 32.

God is love were believed to be necessary. Again, the popular treatments of Packer and Tozer reveal this very concern.

Moving beyond these speculative philosophical forms of systematic theology required me to revise how I understood many biblical passages about God. This required me to interpret them in ways that we shall see as we go further along.

God and Emotion

For more than twenty years I preached through entire books of the Bible as a pastor. One thing this expositional method did was to force me to wrestle deeply with the Scripture. I would normally not have questioned my own theological presuppositions unless I had experienced the Bible profoundly working its way into my mind and heart. (I was trained to trust the Bible, thus this has always been the case.) As I searched the Scriptures week by week, I saw God's love frequently expressed "as a passionate love, complete with joy in human successes and suffering in compassion over human failure."[12] I saw this to be true when I preached through Genesis and several Old Testament prophets even though my theology did not yet allow me to explore this in any depth. I especially saw it in preaching from the Psalms. It was even more clear to me when I preached the Gospel of John, the First Epistle of John, Matthew 5–7 and Paul's letters to the Ephesians, Philippians, and Colossians. This preaching discipline eventually opened my heart to this idea that God does have *real* emotions. But this did not make God weak or unreliable. "Much of the difference between these two theological perspectives centers upon the following question: Must the God perfect in love suffer with those who suffer or does the highest form of love transcend all disturbances?"[13] Subtly, this question still impacts how many readers will *experience* divine love.

I have come to believe that highly speculative conceptions of God "[were] not so much a positive doctrine about the character of divine life in the minds of many Church Fathers as it was a way of saying that no *emotional imperfections* can be attributed to God (e.g. petty jealousy or fits

---

12. Wessling, *Love Divine*, 114.

13. Wessling, *Love Divine*, 114–15. The answers to these questions are considered from many perspectives and there are excellent surveys of the relevant material that can be found; cf. notes 1 and 2 in Wessling on page 115.

of rage)."[14] Emotions, per se, are not descriptive of God's nature. But I remain unconvinced that impassibility, and related ideas, solve the relevant biblical questions regarding the nature of divine love, a love that suffers.

Does Sin Bring Sorrow to God?

The insights of Orthodox theologian Kallistos Ware again prove helpful. "Does our sin cause sorrow to the heart of God? Does he suffer when we suffer? Do we have the right to say to a man or woman who is suffering: 'God himself, at this very moment, is suffering what you suffer, and is overcoming it?'"[15] I am now convinced that we can and should say this.

Ware, certainly not a liberal theologian, reasoned in this way: "the early Fathers, Greek and Latin, insisted on the 'impassability' of God. 'Strictly interpreted' this means that while God-made-man (i.e. Jesus) can and does suffer, God in himself does not. Without denying the Patristic teaching should we not also say something more than this?" Ware notes that Judges 10:16 clearly says: "His soul was grieved for Israel."[16] (Jeremiah 31:20 and Hosea 11:8 underscore this same truth.)

> If these passages mean anything at all, they must mean that even before the incarnation God is directly involved in the sufferings of his creation. Our misery causes grief to God; the tears of God are joined to those of man. A proper respect for the apophatic approach will, of course, make us wary of ascribing human feelings to God in a crude or unqualified way.[17]

If we use impassibility to understand the divine attributes I believe we end up with several soul-numbing abstractions. I believe this is a major disaster for most popular theology. Such theological abstractions can produce a culture of fear, loathing, and rejection.

Eventually I came to see that *sheer transcendence* was more like *sheer otherness*, a profound linguistic and philosophical impossibility. The Christian gospel, as we've already seen, clearly says that God is "other" than the world. He is the Creator. But as we've also seen it just as clearly

---

14. Jordan Wessling, *Love Divine: A Systematic Account of God's Love for Humanity*, citing Paul Gavrilyuk, who argued that this idea of passibility is not radically far from patristic teaching about God.

15. Ware, *The Orthodox Way*, 63.

16. Ware, *The Orthodox Way*, 63.

17. Ware, *The Orthodox Way*, 63.

says God is *never alien* to this world. *He is deeply and personally present and involved.* Bonhoeffer was right—God in Jesus Christ is "the man who lives out of the transcendent."[18]

If what I am saying could be summed up in one word it would have to be the Hebrew word *Immanuel*, which literally means "God with us." This, of course, was the very name given to Jesus! Though he is *other*, he is personally *related* to every one of us because he is always for us and with us. He is, as Barth said, the divine "Yes." Nothing escapes God's love because nothing escapes the one who is God-Love.

The Meaning of Providence

Closely related to the idea that God suffers with us is the doctrine of providence, "Why did God *send* suffering?" This question came from a friend suffering cancer while I was writing this chapter. My response was one of anguish: "I do not believe God *sent* this cancer." I came to this conclusion by rethinking the biblical teaching on divine providence. I now believe the true meaning of providence is this—God is neither responsible for the evils we suffer nor does God shield us from suffering and evil. God does *not* send disaster, nor does God always protect us against disaster. Instead the God of love is *with us* in all our suffering. In dark times God inspires us to embrace his love as we struggle to live with hope. Terence Fretheim states succinctly what I now see in the Bible: "God is believed to be everywhere present yet God will be especially present in certain places."[19]

For the Christian the cross is where we go to gain a better understanding of God-Love. Romans 8:35–39 is as clear as any text in the Bible. From the cross, both on the historic hill outside of Jerusalem and the cross that runs through the heart of our Father, we can see that Jesus loves, forgives, and reconciles. "Force, authority, and prestige are all rendered powerless by the cross."[20]

Love Must Be Grounded in Who God Is

The history of biblical studies and theology gives us significant warnings about placing an *unspecified emphasis on the love of God*. When this is

---

18. Phillips, *Christ for Us in the Theology of Dietrich Bonhoeffer*, see 77–80.
19. Fretheim, *Suffering of God*, 62.
20. Evely, *Rejoice!*, 40.

done, as it is has been done in much popular preaching, the gospel is turned into a naïve belief in inevitable progress or prosperity. This message goes something like this—God loves me, thus nothing bad will happen to me if I trust him! Far too many Christians have embraced the affirmation that God *always* provides what they need if they only trust him. Those who reason this way point to God's love but they miss the robust view of God-Love we've seen in Scripture. This type of preaching and psychology has influenced generations of conservative Protestant Christians who now embrace ideas that are plainly unfaithful to the Scripture.[21]

But as considerable as these difficulties are we must not turn away from a healthy understanding of God-Love. This tragic misrepresentation means we must tell the whole story of divine love much better. Why? The story the Scripture tells, as well as the historical experience of the church, compels us to freely speak of God as love. This has to be a major reason why John 3:16 has meant so much to Christians. This wonderful summary of God's purpose stands firm—1 John 4:8 is merely a simple summary statement of the biblical narrative when it says: "God is love."

I conclude: "It is love that characterizes God's inner life, and it is love that shapes God's dealings with humanity."[22] But can we know and experience this love or are we left in the dark trying to understand it?

> ... we are not totally in the dark about what God's love is. On the contrary, we can reason about God's love with some measure of accuracy precisely because God has created us to imitate His love, and even participate in it.... [When we reflect] upon the nature of God's love for us ... [we see] that God responds to our dignity by valuing our existence and flourishing as well as union with us. This love is an affective love that rests upon each and everyone of us. Indeed, we were created for the purpose of being loved and God never strays from his initial creative purpose, even in his most hellish punishments.... For the Christian, then, it is as Love that we are to obey, praise, and love God.[23]

It has been said that there was a cross in the heart of God before there was a cross on a hill outside Jerusalem. Though the cross on the hill can no longer be seen the cross that is in God's heart remains. "It is the

---

21. This type of preaching is spreading widely in Africa and elsewhere. Preachers promise hearers that they can have what they ask for—health, prosperity and success—if they only believe.
22. Wessling, *Love Divine*, 247.
23. Wessling, *Love Divine*, 247.

cross of pain and triumph—both together. And those who can believe this will find that joy is mingled with their cup of bitterness. They will share on a human level in the divine experience of victorious suffering."[24]

A Better Understanding of God's Transcendence

We saw in the previous chapter that the Bible consistently appeals to transcendence when describing God. *God is eternity itself.* But hundreds of texts tell us that God is immanent as well. Does this truth of transcendence mean God is timeless, or outside of time? Classical Christian theism has generally claimed this to be the case by saying God is *outside of time*. (If you want to stir up a Sunday school class or small group, suggest that God is *not* timeless. Be prepared to be called a heretic!) This standard view of time claims that *simultaneously* everything is before the eyes of God. Once again, this thinking entered into Christian theology through Greek ideas that regarded time as *imperfection*. Hebrew thought did not see time in this way at all. The Old Testament regards time and history as *the framework* for God's loving action. Many Christian theologians have begun to see this truth more clearly, so they now seek to deconstruct the Greek influence that tended to depersonalize God.[25]

What all this means is that the Bible does not provide us with rigidly philosophical answers to questions such as: "Is God timeless?" Or, "Where is God?" Or, "What is God like?" No doubt philosophy has a role to play in interpreting how truth works, but we must understand that the Bible primarily addresses far more important questions, such as: "What does God require of us?" Or, "How shall I give thanks for what God has done for us?" The "us" here is the biblical word used to point to the reality that God treats us as part of his creational community of love. Here, once again, we see how sin affects all we do.

When we speak of where God is, and who God is, we are speaking of divine transcendence *without* necessarily knowing God. The commentary of a Russian Orthodox theologian has helped me here.

> This is the most striking thing about the religion of revelation: God remains under the veil of mystery and yet at the same time he is so close to people that they can call him "our God" and "my God." It is here that we encounter the gulf between divine

---

24. Ware, *Orthodox Way*, 64.
25. Olson, "Example of Unwarranted Theological Speculation."

revelation and the achievements of human thought: the God of the philosophers remains abstract and lifeless, whereas the God of revelation is a living, close and personal God. Both ways lead us to understand that God is incomprehensible and true mystery: yet philosophy abandons us at the foothills of the mountain, forbidding us to ascend further, whereas religion leads us up to the heights where God abides in darkness, it draws us into the cloud of unknowing where beyond all words, and rational deductions, it opens up before us the mystery of God.[26]

The God of the Hellenistic philosophers was a self-contained absolute being who had no deficiency. "The God of the Bible is . . . radically transcendent over nature and history, but he willed to enter human history in order to direct it to super-historical ends."[27]

He's Got the Whole World in His Hands

The unlimited presence, knowledge, and influence of God have often been summarized in this single word I keep using: *transcendence*. Gregory of Nazianzus said: "God is utterly transcendent."[28] The God who is love has always been incomparably present in our midst and he has never abandoned the world.[29]

This question of transcendence ultimately leads us to see the importance of God's immanence, i.e., God is always "with us." Immanence means God is pervading and sustaining the entire universe. He is not an *absentee landlord. God is always active in presence. This activity should be understood as one of eternal love.* Athanasius and Aquinas both rightly said the God who is holy is with us by "palpably indwelling the human world."[30] This divine life defies most comparisons. The holy One of Israel is "among you" (Isa 12:6) and he is an intimate partner in dialog (Isa 12:3). God remains "everywhere at home, every moment engaged, ceaselessly involved in the world. No one is a stranger to this all-present God who shows His love and justice through the events of human history (Isa. 5)."[31]

---

26. Alfayev, *Mystery of Faith*, 11.
27. Bloesch, *God the Almighty*, 208.
28. Oden, *Classic Christianity*, cited on page 54.
29. There are many ways Christians have explained and defended this idea but in the end they confess that God is always with us.
30. Cited by Oden, *Classic Christianity*, 54.
31. Oden, *Classic Christianity*, 54.

It has taken me a long time to clearly see this biblical relationship between divine transcendence and immanence. I submit that you should begin to read the whole story of God's love and grace with these truths firmly fixed in your mind.

> The immanent and transcendent God of Israel is immersed in the space and time of this world; this God is available to all, is effective along with them at every occasion, and moves with them into an uncertain future.[32] Such a perspective reveals a divine vulnerability, as God takes on all the risks that authentic relatedness entails. Because of what happens in that relationship with those whom God loves, God suffers.[33]

St. Paul plainly saw this truth. "The God who made the world and everything in it, he who is Lord of heaven and earth, does not live in shrines made by human hands" (Acts 17:24). But Paul said this utterly transcendent Creator is very close to us: ". . . so that they [we] would search for God and perhaps fumble about for him and find him—though indeed he is not far from each one of us" (Acts 17:27).

Love is Self-Surrender

Hans Urs von Balthasar wrote some of the best theology of God-Love I have ever read. For him *love was always self-surrender* because *the essence of God is self-surrender*. Let this truth pry open your heart. The God who is over all, and in all, is indeed transcendent *and* immanent *in love*. It is his nature to surrender himself because of love. He is not known through psychedelics or trances. He is human and he was seen and witnessed to by persons who gave their lives to follow his message of love.

Suppose we were to further define love as *being and doing for the other* what the other truly needs. In this case divine love is the pattern for all truly human love. And this means God-Love suffers with us. But why? "Since God so loved us, we ought also to love one another" (1 John 4:11).

---

32. This idea of an "uncertain future" that "takes on risks" raises the question sometimes called "God's Openness." Terence Fretheim, the author of this quote, is arguing that real relatedness requires some account of uncertainty. This idea suggests that because God leaves the future open he does not know everything in advance or real decisions we make would be fixed. Some theologians call this "openness theology." This is not the place to argue the pros and cons of this idea but suffice it to say that this is worth considering. It is not heresy, as some evangelicals insist.

33. Fretheim, *Suffering of God*, 78.

Indeed, there is clearly a sense in which divine love must become human love for us to know God's love. Thus there is a way in which the latter is identical with the former, because it is the former that is enabled by the Spirit to become the latter through God's action. "If we love one another, God lives in us and his love is made complete in us" (1 John 4:12). God is with us in God-Love so that we can experience love and share it. I suggest the Scriptures clearly indicate that we will be judged on the basis of a life of love known and shared.

Chapter Eight

A Theology of Love

> Theology is always in progress, but it is ever beginning
> from, and ending in, the greatest mystery of God's love.
>
> —Anthony J. Kelly

> As our principal analogy for God, love can and should serve as a
> critical principle that helps to distinguish good theology from bad.
>
> —Gary Chartier

> What is the place of the love of God in systematic theology?
> Will it serve as a linchpin to maintain the status quo, or will
> it provide critical leverage for a paradigm revolution?
>
> —Kevin Vanhoozer

In my late twenties I embraced a conservative expression of Reformed theology often associated with what some call Calvinism, or "the young, the restless, and the Reformed." By my fortieth birthday I had begun (privately at first) to doubt some of the ways biblical truth was arranged by this paradigm.[1] In my particular context I intellectually knew that God loved me. But eventually my theological conclusions caused me to struggle with the question: "How do I *know* that God *really* loves me?" As I read the Scriptures with an open mind I had to face the truth of God's unbounded love.[2]

The more I understood God-Love as the best way to express the character of God, the more I saw a fresh *reforming principle* working in me. I became increasingly disappointed with much academic evangelical theology, especially where it became obvious that philosophy had a deleterious affect on our understanding of the nature of God. I saw how the doctrine of election, for example, was used to explain away God-Love for *all people*. The idea is that God truly loves some people (thus unto salvation) while he loves other people far less (those who are not the elect thus not loved unto salvation).[3]

Scholasticism and Western Theology

It is commonly agreed that the word "theology" means "thinking about God." (The word comes from two Greek words: (1) *theos*, which means God; and (2) *logos*, which means word. Theology attempts to make sense of what God has revealed by using human reason in trying to understand the Scriptures. (Thus theology is a human work and is never infallible.) In practice theology usually means studying the sources of Christian belief like the Bible and the creeds, as well as exploring the meaning of Christianity for today. I am using the word in this wider sense of "the meaning of Christianity for today." In my evangelical background we thought of theology in four categories: biblical, historical, systematic, and practical. But in

---

1. I remain a minister of Word and sacrament in the Reformed Church in America. As an ecumenist, with ecumenism embraced by my denomination for almost a century, I now see the word "Reformed" as an excellent description of the good faith commitment needed for the continual reforming of the church. ("Reformed and always reforming!") This perspective gives me great confidence that theology, a thoroughly human enterprise, can mature in significant ways.

2. In my experience a great deal of the preaching and reading I did kept one question before me almost every day: "How can I be sure that I am one of the elect?" Encouragement to examine my life for the "evidence of saving grace" did not work.

3. There are numerous debates in church history about this subject. The tension is clear: if God is in *total control* of all things, and God is *eternal*, then God cannot love all persons in the same way. He is love but his love cannot be other than one attribute among many. Another word or metaphor can better explain God's nature than love. Some suggest that word is holy. Others that this attribute is sovereignty.

embracing a theology of love I came to see something that was desperately missing in my theological education—namely, spiritual theology.

Christianity is a historical faith that seeks to persuade us to live in a certain way: the way of love. To be a Christ-follower means that you inherit a particular tradition whether you know it or not. Tradition as a living faith calls us to receive the witness of Israel, the story of Jesus, and the witness of Christians who followed Jesus. This means our faith must be more than acknowledging facts. It must become a way of life rooted in the One who is "the way, the truth and the life" (John 14:6). *This way requires a continual retrieval of the spiritual life of the Christian community.* We must avoid becoming smug and satisfied with secondhand faith.

In the Western church a medieval approach to philosophy (1100–1700) arose that profoundly influenced the way theology was done in the academy.[4] This approach, usually called scholasticism, was clearly indebted to the rediscovery of the works of Aristotle. Scholasticism was used to harmonize Aristotle's ideas with a great deal of Trinitarian theology. Various monastic schools in the West adopted this method in order to give a reasonable account of God and his works. "To make a long and complicated story short, as scholasticism took over in the teaching of Christian doctrine, the logical patterns essential to Aristotelian thought also became dominant."[5]

Initially the Protestant Reformation challenged Latin Catholic scholastic thought, yet the method itself remained strong. It was eventually used by both Lutheran and Reformed traditions. This pattern continued until the end of the nineteenth century. The teaching of theologians such as Philip Melancthon (Lutheran) and Theodore Beza (Reformed) used scholastic categories to compile a written theology drawing from Luther and Calvin.[6] While it is incorrect to say that scholasticism *is* theology (since it really is a method) this method had immense influence for centuries. Scholasticism profoundly shaped a growing confessional Protestant theology that had a role in how I first understood my own theology.

In Catholic theology the greatest scholastic thinker was undoubtedly Thomas Aquinas. Thomas, a rare person in church history since we designate him simply by his first name, produced a *comprehensive*

---

4. Most historians of theology agree that Anselm was the father of this approach.

5. Payton Jr., *Getting the Reformation Wrong,* 45.

6. It is widely debated how this scholastic approach influenced Calvin and Luther. I do not think either fully embraced the approach but the second and third generation of Protestants clearly did use this way for ordering theology.

A Theology of Love

synthesis of Christian theology using Aristotelian philosophy. This may have been the greatest such system ever written. His method has influenced formal Roman Catholic thought for centuries. (His thinking was adopted as the official philosophy of the church in 1917.) Vatican II began a modest movement away from *rigid* dependence on Thomas, yet revivals of interest continue through what is called neo-Thomism. Thomas still profoundly influences Catholic theologians. "While scholastic theology did not follow Aristotle in affirming certain ideas that could not be found in Scripture the ancient philosopher's stress on logic and rationality became the unquestioned norm."[7]

In my own reforming process, especially in embracing God-Love, I soon realized how this scholastic method shaped my own thinking. Anselm, called the father of scholasticism, put forward his most famous idea with three simple words: "faith seeking understanding." The irony of this thesis should not be lost. The so-called father of scholasticism warned against the dangers of using a philosophical method to *explain* God rather than the faith itself. James R. Payton Jr. summarizes this well: "The scholastic pattern was to run everything through this grid with the result that the basic premise of the particular scholastic theologian dominated the whole package of his thought and teaching."[8] Initially I did not realize that I had adopted such a system through which I put Scripture into logical categories.

Hendrikus Berkhof helped me embrace my love-centric theology by suggesting we must understand the *contrast* between *relationship* and *objectification*. "'*Faith*' is a relationship, '*study*' or exposition is an *objectifying activity*; consequently the study of the faith looks very much like a contradiction in terms. A love relationship can be experienced; it can also be studied; but can one ever do both at the same time?"[9] This is the kind of helpful insight that struck at the heart of what I had done with theology for years.

I now believe a *reverent contemplation* of the object of our affection (God) is necessary for good theology. However, attempts to intellectually *master* theology run the profound risk of turning God into the object for our study that Berkhof warned against. Right thinking about God is good but it must arise out of an encounter with the God who is love. This encounter must lead us to *know* God as our end, not as a rational

---

7. Payton Jr., *Getting the Reformation Wrong*, 45.
8. Payton Jr., *Getting the Reformation Wrong*, 45.
9. Berkhof, *Christian Faith*, 30.

explanation. The process of knowing God clearly involves the intellect but it requires far, far more. It requires true and careful thought, but this thought depends wholly on the Spirit. The intellect must become the *faithful servant* of a deep relationship.

Hendrikus Berkhof put forward the idea that the study of the Christian faith (theology) is "a systematic examination of the contents of the relationship which God in Christ has entered into with us."[10] This type of understanding avoids both subjectivist and objectivist understandings of theology.

Greek Ideas

The second challenge to a healthy theology of God-Love comes from several Greek ideas that I've already cited. Biblical theologians often saw God's essence expressed in his name, the name that was first given in the Pentateuch. "There is one concept which seems one-sidedly to express God's sovereignty . . . the Hebrew *kābôb* and the Greek *doxa* . . . both translated 'glory' and sometimes 'honor.' The theological insight into this unity of transcendence and condescendence, by and large, became a lost theme in the history of the church."[11] In the process of losing this theme something happened to our understanding of God because of this *overemphasis* on Greek philosophy. (This is a double-edged sword, if you please. Greek ideas served the theology of the church well in some important ways.) Let me explain this point as clearly as possible.

Greek thinking saw the divine as high and far away. Plato, for example, saw God as *the highest ideal*, the true ideal of the good. For Plato God was "beyond being." Aristotle said God was "a perfect being," thus "thinking which thinks itself, the unmoved prime mover." Neo-Platonism called God "the first." These variations on the nature of who God is provided an intellectual bridge for Christian theology but these ideas also came to shape the way Christians sought to explain God.

Philo of Alexandria (25 BCE–40 CE), a brilliant Hellenistic Jewish thinker, said God is "the one who is." The problem with this should be apparent at this point. Instead of seeing God as a *relational being of love* Christian theology began to think of God as "imperishable, unchangeable

---

10. Berkhof, *Christian Faith*, 33.

11. Berkhof, *Christian Faith*, 107. I am deeply indebted to Berkhof, a twentieth-century Dutch theologian, who explained this in a way that should cause Reformed theology to become more "reforming."

and invisible."[12] Here the intellectual beginning of the idea of divine "attributes" took shape, thus the "omni" words about God's nature came to be commonly used, e.g., omnipotent, omnipresent, omniscient. As we've already seen these ancient ideas shaped later confessions and catechisms. They also shaped the theology of the Catholic Church for centuries. At Vatican I (1868–69) God was defined as "mighty, eternal, immense, incomprehensible, infinite in his intellect and will in all perfection. As he is one unique and spiritual substance, entirely simple and unchangeable, we must proclaim him distinct from the world in existence and essence, blissfully in himself and from himself, ineffably exalted above all things that exist or can be conceived besides him."[13] I submit it is very difficult to see God as deeply personal and relational in such words. Vatican II sought to open a door to a richer and more love-centric understanding of God.

Thankfully the use of these Greek thoughts did not wholly shape the faith of the church. Berkhof correctly observes that the church, both Catholic and Protestant, has "an entirely different vocabulary, the one used in sermons, liturgies, hymns, and meditations, which speak not only of God's transcendence, but are also filled with praise for God's condescendence. Dogmatics, however, saw this latter aspect as limited to the area of revelation and not as belonging to the essence of God."[14] Formal theology still fails to see how the practice of believers belongs to a *theology of the essence of God*. This may have been one reason why scholastic and speculative ideas about God kept my heart from understanding God as love. The doctrine of God must be released from these abstract and sterile notions. But doing so will challenge some highly cherished ideas.

I am not alone in saying that the theology of God in the West became increasingly abstract. Thankfully hymns and liturgies did play a huge role in keeping me centered in love. As I hope you can see, the God-Love theology I now embrace is anything but abstract. This theology seeks the glory of knowing God as the love of my life, indeed my dearest friend (John 15:13–15).[15]

---

12. This can be seen in Aristides (140 CE), who used such words to describe the nature of God.

13. Quoted from the documents of Vatican I, Berkhof, *Christian Faith*, 108.

14. Berkhof, *Christian Faith*, 108–9.

15. I will explore a "friendship motif" in John's Gospel in another chapter. It is safe to say "friendship" does fit with the relationship a disciple can have with God, based on John 15.

Kevin Vanhoozer, one of evangelical Christianity's best contemporary theologians, offers us a succinct and cogent introduction to divine love by giving a wonderful overview of what I call a theology of love.

> What, then, is the place of the love of God in systematic theology? Will it serve as a linchpin to maintain the status quo, or will it provide critical leverage for a paradigm revolution? It is too soon to tell. Perhaps the moral of this . . . is that the love of God should occupy no one place in a theological system, but every place. Instead of trying to situate the love of God under one doctrinal locus, the theologian's task is rather to witness to its inexhaustibility. To write on the love of God is the Christian theologian's supreme privilege and supreme responsibility. In the final analysis, of course, the love of God belongs not only in systematic theology, but in the praise of those who know God's love and who cannot help but witness to it by their lives and loves.[16]

God-Love Theology

What I now call God-Love theology eventually gave me a growing personal confidence in love. I was thirsty and theology did not quench my thirst. I now believe that what is called "confirmation bias" hindered me.[17] I looked for what confirmed my existing ideas. By the time I reached my forties I had written and edited several books and preached widely. Frankly, examining some of my own ideas about God was uncomfortable. I had already lost public support for embracing a vision I called "missional-ecumenism." Furthermore, I did not want to offend friends who had invited me to share with their churches. I submit that confirmation bias is far too common. It is human nature to avoid crossing the lines we've drawn around our ideas. But when these ideas are about the nature of God things become even more challenging.

What I finally came to see was that "doctrinal definitions can tell us truths about God but only contemplation can bring us immediate, personal, and direct experiential knowledge of God."[18]

---

16. Vanhoozer, ed., *Nothing Greater, Nothing Better*, 29.

17. Confirmation bias is a psychological term for the human tendency to seek out only information that supports one position or idea. This causes you to have a bias towards your original position because if you only seek out information that supports one idea, you will only find information that supports that idea.

18. Bartos, *Deification in Eastern Theology*, 35.

Calvin and Calvinism

Martin Luther initially helped me in balancing God's power with his grace and goodness. Yet over time I found Reformed theology to be a more robust assessment of my own biblical faith. (I now realize you can marshal texts from the Bible for almost any theological system.) I am persuaded that we must admit that the goal of careful biblical understanding is not to line up texts to support our view. Some seem to think you can solve the problem of multiple texts, that appear to say different things, by using a compilation method.

Louis Berkhof, a twentieth century conservative Reformed theologian, wrote a systematic theology of 992 pages. In this massive book he never explored *a* single reference to the divine love passages of the Bible. I find this incredible! The publisher's website says of this book: "[It] has remained the most influential twentieth-century compendium of Reformed theology."

Louis Berkhof was just being consistent with the thinking of scholastic Calvinism. Calvin's hugely influential book, *The Institutes of the Christian Religion* (a work of over 1,800 pages in one modern reprinting), is truly a classic. I find it surprising that Calvin never mentions the three texts on love we saw in 1 John 4. Calvin's work provides what some believe to be the best summary of Christian doctrine ever composed. (In the modern Westminster Press edition, there are thirty-nine pages of biblical texts listed in the appendix. These are printed in three columns per page. That's a lot of Bible verses!) Amazingly Calvin "did not even find it important enough to explain away" these texts on love![19]

The more I read theology books the more I returned to my treasured Yale University Press volumes of the works of Jonathan Edwards. When Edwards contemplated the relationship of God with the redeemed in heaven he wrote: "The Apostle tells us that God is love, 1 John 4:8. And therefore seeing he is an infinite Being, it follows that he is full and overflowing and an inexhaustible fountain of love. Seeing he is an unchangeable and eternal Being, he is an unchangeable and eternal source of love."[20] Wow! Edwards clearly embraced a step in the right direction. His words pushed me further as I sought to see what the love of God meant. But this is *not* the whole story of Edwards' theology of God. (It is rightly noted that Edwards preached more on love than he did on sin or hell.)

---

19. Talbott, *Inescapable Love of God*, 104.
20. Edwards, *Charity and Its Fruits*, 369.

When Jonathan Edwards contemplated God's relationship with those who were outside of Christ he concluded: "In hell God manifests his Being and perfections only in hatred and wrath, and hatred *without love*."[21] How could this be? It eventually proved exceptionally hard for me to process this idea. Only after further searching would I see Edwards's most *unhelpful* idea about God.

> By "hatred without love" he evidently meant an attitude quite incompatible with love. So at this point, the question arises, how are we to reconcile the second quotation with the first? Suppose Edwards had said in one place that God's righteousness is "infinite," "inexhaustible," "unchangeable" and "eternal," and then had said in another that God acts towards some people—say, the non-elect or the members of some minority race—in some expedient way *without righteousness*. That would have posed a similar problem of interpretation. How could God's righteousness be both infinite and eternal if it is also limited in the sense that he sometimes acts without righteousness? And similarly, one wonders, how could God be an infinite, inexhaustible, overflowing, and eternal source of love if his love is also limited in the sense that he acts sometimes without love?[22]

Once I saw these contradictions I had a problem. Either I would have to humbly walk back some of my earlier understanding, and embrace a different way of thinking about the nature of God, or I would throw up my hands in utter confusion. I chose to press on trying to understand how God was perfect love and what this meant for divine justice and wrath.

What or *Who*?

Not long after I embraced the teaching commonly called Calvinism I was introduced to the *Westminster Confession and Shorter Catechism*. In many ways this confession and catechism helped me more than anything I had previously been taught. A stark opposition to creeds and catechisms in my background was altered by these documents. But this is also where I got into deep weeds regarding the love of God. It took me nearly two decades to see where I had gone wrong.

The *Westminster Shorter Catechism* says:

21. Edwards, *Charity and Its Fruits*, 390.
22. Talbott, *Inescapable Love of God*, 105.

Question 4. What is God?

Answer: God is a Spirit, infinite, eternal, and unchangeable in his being, wisdom, power, holiness, justice, goodness, and truth.

I do not desire to completely debunk this answer. There is obviously a great deal about it that is good. But several things really do trouble me.

We might immediately object, in what sense should we ask *"what"* is God? If God is *personal*, and almost all Christians agree he is, then why ask "What"? God creates and redeems. His relationship with us is actively situated love. *But why? The obvious answer is that God loves us personally and relationally.* Jesus made this abundantly clear. Second, if God made us because of love, and sends his Son to live and die for us as perfect love, then God is not "what." God is who, a who that is truly good! It is a right understanding of God's goodness which inspires love in us. *God's loving nature is a wonder to behold.* I thus came to believe that divine love was the true basis for a deep, life-changing standard of true human goodness.[23]

Our Western Understanding of God Needs the East

Having grown up in the Christian West, and having been taught the theology of Protestantism in particular, it took me time to see that God was fundamentally incomprehensible. This discovery led me to have far less confidence in some of the propositional affirmations I learned. (I think here of theories of the atonement and understanding divine election, as just two examples.) Why? Orthodoxy actively embraces "divine incomprehensibility." This approach never loses sight of our finitude and God's transcendence. (Perhaps this will help you see why I make a great deal out of transcendence in this book.) This approach will make room for cataphatic theology, or negation. Here the "inevitable limitations of all our propositional affirmations about God" can help us stop fighting one another over our particular articulations of the faith.[24] (I am *not* suggesting we deny the core truth of the creeds.) This discovery proved immensely helpful in living out my ecumenical vision.[25]

---

23. I realize there is an archaic sense in which the "what" in this question can be a substitute for "who" but I think in modern use this question hardly helps us contemplate God's nature as perfect love.

24. Payton Jr., *Light from the Christian East*, 84.

25. See my books, especially *Costly Love*, to engage with my vision of Christian oneness.

My Western background in evangelicalism was filled with controversies about interpreting the Bible in certain ways. As an example, I was once told by a department head that if I explicitly taught my ancient-faith understanding of the atonement I might not been allowed to continue teaching. In another instance my understanding of how our various theories about biblical inspiration created a tension, as did my understanding of the fall. (And these are only three such responses.)

> Apophatic theology undercuts the presumption that we limited human beings—via reading Scripture, studying doctrine and using our minds—have become experts in talking about God because we have mastered the data of revelation. We do not have, and must not act as if we have "God in a box," whether that box be denominational or doctrinal. Beyond what we claim to know and understand, beyond all our limitations, is our God—who invites us to leave behind our considerable intellection and to encounter him beyond our capacities.[26]

Is God Personal?

As I have mentioned, an ancient philosopher who had a profound influence on developing Christian thought was Plato. Plato's thought has been called a "dualism of appearance and reality, of change and permanence, of opinion and knowledge, of body and soul, and of earthly 'copies' or 'images.'" In Plato's view the world yields "mere copies" of that which is real. In this view "the eternal One, as eternal God, is characterized by changeless Being."[27] Ideas like these depersonalize God and become central to knowing God. As much as Plato helped some Christians form significant ideas they discovered in the Scripture, the end result of this approach falls short of the rich biblical message about God as unadulterated love.

Earlier I suggested that we need to understand that God is truly *personal*. But what does *personal* really mean? Am I saying God is a human person just like us?

> A personal relationship involves and requires an interactive speaking and listening relationship of free beings. Even though God's way of being a person far transcends human ways of being persons, nonetheless the divine-human encounter is portrayed

---

26. Payton Jr., *Light from the Christian East*, 86.
27. Thiselton, *Concise Encyclopedia of the Philosophy of Religion*, 230–31.

in Scripture as a personal relationship of meeting, communication, becoming mutually committed, experiencing frustrations and failure, splitting up, and becoming reconciled again (cf. Exodus 28:43; Numbers 11:33; 1 Samuel 10:1–5; Psalm 4:; 17:1; 74:1; Hosea 14:1; Irenaeus, *Against Heresies* 2:1). All of these are things that happen to persons.[28]

As we saw earlier, we do not commit ourselves to a "giant-in-the-sky," or "the Man Upstairs." This language of the personal takes into account "the symbolic language of revelation."[29] This symbolic language leads us to a significant analogy, namely this: the God who is love always meets us in our personhood. *God is infinitely higher than we are but when we meet him it is always in a profoundly personal context.*

But is Love a Single Theme in Scripture?

In *Nothing Greater, Nothing Better,* Kevin Vanhoozer says there are nuances in how modern Protestants try to construct a theology of love; thus the ten essays of his excellent collection do not provide a single "definitive response" to the questions that surround our subject. But in the Introduction Vanhoozer says if one tried to see a "single theme" it would have to be "that it is not human love per se, but rather the love of the man Jesus—representative both of God and of an authentic humanity—that is the ultimate criterion for thinking about the love of God."[30] With this careful response I now agree.

---

28. Oden, *Classic Christianity,* 55–56.
29. Berkhof, *Christian Faith,* 130.
30. Vanhoozer, ed., *Nothing Better, Nothing Greater,* 24.

Chapter Nine

Is Love All We Need?

> Love is not merely an outward mark and symbol of His presence, but His very self in action in our world.
>
> —John Baillie

> God is He who sees with the eyes of love, by whose seeing things are enabled to be themselves, by whose seeing I am enabled to be myself.
>
> —Romano Guardini

I CAME OF AGE in the turbulent sixties. In the summer of 1967 the Beatles first sang John Lennon's popular song "All You Need is Love." My generation sang along.

> All you need is love
> All you need is love
> All you need is love, love
> Love is all you need.

Was John Lennon right? Many conservative Christians attacked the Beatles and their songs by saying they were godless, confused young men. They even said the lyrics of this song were silly, if not dangerous. Really? These words did not ignite a robust discussion about God's love but they did open a door for Christians to share the truth of divine love. Popular culture often has a tendency to do this if we pay attention.

In the last chapter we saw why it is extremely difficult to develop a comprehensive theology of love. Perhaps this difficulty is one reason Christian scholars have put forward so many different ways for understanding the nature of God. I must make one thing clear: I am not attacking Christians who disagree with any part of my thesis. In fact, some of the very best Christians scholars and teachers I have ever known hold at least some of the views I have come to question. What I am doing is inviting us into a new/ancient conversation about the nature of God.

A Simple Primer

At this point it should be obvious that I have not solved all of the problems we face in constructing a theology of God-Love. I am only offering a simple primer on how such a theology can proceed. What I have tried to do is give you a demonstration of *how* this truth makes the entire biblical story life-changing. It centers on the Bible's own story, on who God really is in his person.

I hope by now you can see that God-Love is not simply a *particular system*. We have writers and theologians, in both the Eastern and the Western Church—Protestant, Catholic, Orthodox, Pentecostal and evangelical—who all affirm divine love in a wide variety of ways. A growing number of modern theologians have been pioneers in recovering what we've seen to this point. You might observe, through my various footnotes, that I believe Orthodoxy frames this theology best by giving us a robust understanding of divine love.

Plato and Platonism

In the previous chapter we saw how scholastic theology and Greek ideas both helped create a system whereby the knowledge of God was shrouded in categories that I have suggested are sub-biblical. Various extra-biblical words have been employed by theologians to describe God (e.g., words such as impassible, omniscient, omnipotent). These words became prominent in much theology. Thus theology, taught in academic settings, influenced pastors as well as their sermons and books.

Plato influenced the theology of the church early in its history. His thought retains a formative influence to this day. "Whatever Plato's influence on Christian thought may have been, especially from the second century to the fifth, there has never been, and cannot be, a 'Christian Plato' in the full sense of these two words. The only valid statement to be made is that of Pascal's: 'Plato, dispose[d] people toward Christianity.'"[1]

In some ways Plato actually had an even bigger influence on Christianity than Aristotle. The influence of his ideas impacted prominent thinkers. But why does this matter to our quest to develop a theology of God-Love? Plato's influence separated the Hebrew Scripture and experience from the thoughts of the New Testament itself. Here is but one example—his idea of immortality. This development still informs popular ideas about God, particularly in the soul/body distinction and various popular ideas about what happens to us when we die. Justin Martyr spoke of moving from Stoicism to Aristotle until he met a Platonist whose "perception of immaterial things ... furnished my mind with wings."[2] Augustine of Hippo praised Plato's account of nonmaterial reality and said he gave to the church a limited but useful natural theology. Tertullian, on the other hand, declared open hostility to Plato's philosophy.

There are a number of ways in which I could show you how Plato and Platonism adversely influenced theology. "Traditionally, in older works, God's omnipotence, omnipresence, and omniscience are often called 'his metaphysical attributes.'" The term "attributes," so widely employed by conservative Christians today, actually suggests "a relation to the vocabulary of Greek philosophy rather than the Bible."[3]

I cannot explore this in depth so one negative connotation must suffice. An internet explanation of God's omnipotence says this word refers to God's sovereignty, which speaks to God's right to do *whatever he wishes*. This was the very idea I embraced by believing that God can and does exercise *control* over *all* events. I now believe this idea should be graciously challenged.

---

1. Des Places, "Platonism and Christianity," in Latourelle and Fisichella, eds., *Dictionary of Fundamental Theology*, 781. This source is a wonderfully full treatment by modern Catholic theologians and historians.

2. Thiselton, *Thiselton Companion to Christian Theology*, 676.

3. Thiselton, *Thiselton Companion to Christian Theology*, 357.

The word "omnipotent" suggests "power over," which very often suggests force. This was how I understood divine sovereignty. I could cite dozens of texts that seemed to support this understanding. A modern Reformed theologian, however, has called this idea of omnipotence "brute force," concluding that "the most shockingly bad of all [ideas] implies enabling and empowering."[4] I find the distinction between *power over* and *power with* immensely helpful. God has power *with* because God is almighty. I do not deny any fundamental truth about God's authority and power but I understand "power with" to be a much better way to explain God's sovereignty.[5]

Final Reconciliation?

The Scriptures plainly tells us that at the end of this age Jesus will complete what he began. Then he will reconcile the whole world to his Father. "For in him all the fullness of God was pleased to dwell, and through him God was pleased to reconcile to himself *all things*, whether on earth or in heaven, by making peace through the blood of his cross" (Col 1:19–20). Acts 3:21 refers to this as the time of "universal restoration" (*apokatastasis*). The end is clearly not a heavenly home far removed from this earth, as so many think. God will redeem the cosmos and make the earth a new Eden. The end will be the consummation of Christ's kingdom on earth, just as Jesus taught us to pray (Matt 6:9–10).

Does this mean that at the end of the age God will finally save all people? The more I have wrestled with the doctrine of God's love the more I have come to see that we must always assert God's universal love. At the same time I believe we must be careful not to assert too much. We must, for example, avoid the idea that God's love is arbitrary. I believe professor David Ferguson is right to allow human beings the freedom to receive divine grace or to reject it when he concludes, "Only a theology that recognizes the freedom finally to rebel against God can avoid the determinism of double predestination or universalism."[6] He argues cogently "that universalism appears to be committed to a theology that is as deterministic and destructive of human freedom as the doctrine of double predestination in hyper-Calvinism. In particular, it does not

---

4. van den Brink, *Almighty God*, 46–60.
5. Thiselton, *Thiselton Companion to Christian Theology*, 357.
6. Ferguson, chapter 9 in Vanhoozer, ed., *Nothing Greater, Nothing Better*, 196.

allow any human being the freedom finally to say 'no' to God. Yet without this possibility can we really be said to have the freedom to finally say 'yes' to God?"[7]

Yet I fully agree with Kallistos Ware when he says we can know two things. God has given us free will and he will never withdraw this freedom from us. This means that it is possible to say "no" to God but it also means that it is possible divine love may well lead all persons to finally and freely choose to say "yes" and accept God's love. "Divine love is inexhaustible. Beyond this we cannot go; but obedient to the words of St. Silouan the Athonite (1866–1938), we 'must pray for all.'"

In chapter 1 we saw how the Christian tradition has seen the story of Moses' encounter with the burning bush as *the flame of God's love and restoring grace*. God's fire draws the whole universe into the circle of his intense love. Thus the light that shines around the saints was not a cool, gentle light but the blazing light of a consuming fire that Christ came to cast upon the earth (Luke 12:49).[8] It is the "living flame of love," as St. John of the Cross said. "It burns and transforms all those whom it touches."[9]

The Deep Cold of Spiritual Winter

In his deeply moving book, *Looking East in Winter*, Rowan Williams shares his personal journey into the spirituality of the Christian East. He suggests that the West now lies in a deep cold of pervasive spiritual winter. I share this sense of where we are. Our problem is far deeper than finding new ways for doing church or being Christians. The myriad solutions that are on offer in the West have failed us. I expect they will continue to fail us. With Rowan Williams I believe we need to look East.[10] Perhaps we just might find profound help in a place that too few of us have ever bothered to look.

---

7. Ferguson, chapter 9 in Kevin J. Vanhoozer, ed., *Nothing Greater, Nothing Better*, 199.

8. If you've looked at many icons you will know that fire/light is often the background to the person represented.

9. Zaleski, *Who Is God?*, 122.

10. Pope John Paul II repeatedly referred to churches of the East and West as "sister churches." He used a beautiful metaphor to express our need to listen and learn from one another by saying the church has "two lungs," East and West. We breathe best when we use both lungs.

There is a particular way that theologians in the Orthodox East approached this subject of naming and speaking of God. In the East theologians generally saw two distinct types of theology that were meant to help disciples be faithful in speaking about God. These two ways have helped me sort our some of the problems in my own theology. These are not Platonic ways; they are profoundly Christian ways. These two ways, which I've briefly mentioned previously, are called cataphatic and apophatic theology. Let's explore these.

Cataphatic Theology and Spirituality

Cataphatic theology, which is *positive* theology, uses *both* positive biblical and philosophical categories to describe God. Much of what we've seen so far involves cataphatic theology. Cataphatic theology uses words, images, and analogies to help us understand God. The Bible clearly demonstrates this type of theology. Furthermore, cataphatic theology embraces the mountain of positive biblical terminology about the being and nature of God. It employs these affirmations in order to help us think more clearly about God. (Most theology in the West, especially Protestant and evangelical theology, has *exclusively* followed this course!)

Apophatic Theology and Spirituality

Apophatic theology, on the other hand, is *negative* theology, i.e., it has been called the *via negativa* (negative way). In the East apophatic theology was employed to express divine truth through negation. *This theology stressed interiority and wordlessness. It emphasized that the transcendent God surpasses human speech and all conceptual or logical expression. It understands God by denying definitions of God.* Apophatic theology, contrary to frequent misconceptions, *complements* cataphatic theology! In this approach we cannot encompass the totality of God's being in our words. So how is this theology helpful?

In the apophatic way Orthodoxy gives us significant cautions. Those who follow only cataphatic theology sometimes feel as if they are caught in a continual struggle with concepts. The apophatic way teaches us how to lose our faith (note: *our* faith, not *the* faith) daily. But why is this important? It will lead us into the unexplainable ways of silence and mystery. I have come to believe that this is where the fire of divine love transforms us through the experience of God-Love.

The more I've used and experienced apophatic spirituality the more I've found that I am often isolated from popular Christianity inside the believing community. When Christians speak of God like "the man upstairs" they have clearly missed the fire of his holy love. In more violent times disciples who embraced this way of negation were labeled as "mystics" and even burnt at the stake.[11]

Apophatic theology has proven to be personally valuable to me in intentionally seeking a deeper experience of God-Love. It has continued to help me see how "not knowing" is a true work of grace. It has also taught me how to listen to various voices in the church.

God's Love Is Intensely Personal

The earliest creed of the Christian church begins with the words: "I believe in God the Father Almighty, Creator of heaven and earth." I submit that this statement is broadly noncontroversial for good reason. Christian theology begins here because, "To believe in creation is to believe that we are here because of God. The activity of God is a *necessary condition* of our existing. And it is to believe that we actually *do* exist, that we are *real*, and not merely figments of the divine imagination."[12]

> God is a communion of persons living in love. And it seems to be the most natural thing in the world (so to speak!) that this communion, in its compassion and joy, wanted to create other people to share in this communion. Love overflows. It gives. So God overflows and gives life to other people to relate to and to love. Humanity is this chosen partner and so is destined for fellowship with God and always has been and always will be. This was the divine intention for humanity "prior to" its creation.[13]

---

11. Williams, *Seeking the God Beyond*, 56.

12. Chartier, *Analogy of Love*, 103.

13. Campbell, *Pauline Dogmatics*, 82. Campbell shows, in 795 pages, how solid biblical theology can be rooted in the overarching narrative of the Bible: "God is love."

The Likeness and Image of God

In creation God planted a desire in us to be united with him in eternal love. Though this "likeness" to God has been defaced, the "image" of God in us remains strong.

Many theologians of the early church, especially in the East, made a *distinction* between image and likeness. I personally find their distinction helpful. The image of God in humanity denotes our *potentiality for life in God* while the divine likeness is *our actual realization of that potentiality*. The image is what we all possess. It enables us to pursue the spiritual way of love. The likeness, however, expresses our hope that we will attain *the fullness of God* at our journey's end. Origen expressed this distinction well: "Man received the honor of the image at his first creation, but the full perfection of God's likeness will only be conferred upon him at the consummation of all things."[14] All of us retain the image of God regardless of how corrupt we might have become. *This means the image of God may be obscured but it is never destroyed.* So we are "image bearers." This is why the picture of "healing" came to dominate much of what the Eastern church fathers understood about our salvation. This restoration of divine likeness was in the future. "Likeness is fully achieved only by the blessed in the heavenly kingdom of the Age to come."[15] St. Irenaeus said that man at his first creation was "as a little child" and needed to "grow" into perfection.[16] (Again, this is a very different understanding of our original position than what we see in some traditional Western views. It also suggests that even *before* the fall we were not mature.)

> This shows how the notion of man as created in God's image can be interpreted in a dynamic rather than a static sense. It need not mean that man was endowed from the outset with a fully realized perfection, and with the highest possible holiness and knowledge, but simply that he was given the opportunity to grow into full fellowship with God.[17]

The idea that we were created to "grow into full fellowship with God" was actually a consensus view in the early church. But this was not how I was taught the human condition. I now believe that humankind

---

14. Origen, *On First Principles III*, vi, I, 245.
15. Ware, *Orthodox Way*, 52.
16. Irenaeus, *Demonstration of the Apostolic Preaching* 12, 81.
17. Ware, *Orthodox Way*, 52.

was created for union with God, not merely to pass a test of obedience. But why? God created persons out of love. "There is no such thing as 'natural man' existing in separation from God: man cut off from God in a highly unnatural state. This image doctrine means, therefore, that man [still] has God at the innermost center of his being."[18] Indeed we are all sinful but we are not *entirely* separated from God. I believe a careful search of the New Testament reveals that we retain a relationship with God. Paul expresses this accordingly: "I bow my knees before the Father, from whom every family in heaven and on earth takes its name" (Eph 3:14–15). Thus "the divine is the determining element in our humanity; losing our sense of the divine, we lose also our sense of the human."[19] Accordingly, the popular idea that sin "separates" us *entirely* from God creates significant problems.

What will help us here is the wonderful metaphor of healing—we desperately need divine healing! We are broken. Though we are not entirely separated from God we are desperately ill and the healing balm of the gospel brings us into *intimate union* with God. This means that any notion that we are totally corrupt trash is just wrong, even desperately wrong! (I heard a lot of this in my early years as a Christian. One popular hymn referred to us all as "worms.") I am now persuaded that being taught that I was "wretched" and separated from God did not help me to really know the love of God. It actually prompted me to embrace my insecurity. It fed into my false understanding of who I really was, a person created and loved by God.

We are beloved persons created for divine love.

Covenant Love

From the creation account, through the call of Abraham and Moses, to the giving of the law to the Israelites, and the call to repentance heralded again and again by the ancient prophets, God displayed covenant love for Israel. This love was always rooted in divine faithfulness. This is what love looks like in the Old Testament.[20] But before you get lost in difficult

---

18. Ware, *Orthodox Way*, 52.
19. Ware, *Orthodox Way*, 52.
20. Christians often miss this truth by neither reading, nor carefully observing, what the Old Testament actually says. Pastors tend not to preach from the Old Testament. The tendency to prooftext doctrines about God is highlighted by how subjects are brought forward and argued by choosing only a few verses, thus missing the "story line" of Israel.

portions of the Old Testament, start with this simple observation—divine love has always been God's plan for all the nations.

> Now the Lord said to Abram, "Go from your country and your kindred and your father's house to the land that I will show you. I will make of you a great nation, and I will bless you and make your name great, so that you will be a blessing. I will bless those who bless you, and the one who curses you I will curse, and *in you all the families of the earth shall be blessed.*" (Gen 12:1–3, italics added)

So what should we make of the claim that divine love can be exaggerated? While there is truth in this type of pushback, "I am of the opinion that we should tread carefully when we suggest ways in which God's love for humanity might be less strong than we otherwise would have thought."[21] I believe we are completely warranted to say that the "God found in the dying face of Christ reveals a love that far exceeds what we would frequently imagine."[22]

Summing up what we've seen in the Hebrew concept of love, we should say that love is God's *active self-giving* (Isa 54:8; Hos 11:1, 2:21–22). The Hebrew words for love warrant us to understand that divine love flows *out of* God's tender mercies. The perfection of divine love, *anticipated cryptically* in the earliest portions of the Old Testament and openly developed by the prophets, was finally and fully revealed in the life, death, and resurrection of the Son of God. This is another reason why John 3:16 is central to the whole biblical story. This is why Hans Urs von Balthasar rightly concludes:

> No one can resolve this mystery into dry concepts and explain how it is that God no longer sees my guilt in me, but only his beloved Son, who bears it for me; or how God sees this guilt transformed through the suffering of love and loves me because I am the one for whom his Son has suffered in love. But the way God, the lover, sees us is in fact the way we are in reality—for God, this is the absolute and irrevocable truth. This is the faith of the Christian. The non-Christian who hears this will begin to think this is too good to be true.[23]

---

21. Wessling, *Love Divine*, 6.
22. Wessling, *Love Divine*, 6.
23. Balthasar, *Love Alone is Credible*, 103.

Embracing Our True Self

The majority of early church theologians believed Adam fell because of his pride. "Pride is the wall that separates humans from God. The root of pride is the state of being turned in on oneself, self-love, lust for oneself."[24] This idea of turning in on oneself reflects how the Christian tradition came to speak of our "true self" and "false self." Our "false self" is the result of our pride. It is our inner desire for importance and approval *without* God. Our "true self" is the result of the love of God given to us in Christ, which gives us everything we need for life and godliness. This means that when we know we are truly loved we can develop and experience a healthy "true self," an inner well-being that progressively restores us to God. We can know that God is love for us. This point is poignantly made by N. T. Wright.

> [God's love for the world; cf. John 3:16] invites us to see the entire drama of creation—the planets, the mountains, the far reaches of cosmic space, the tiniest creature on earth, the refugee, the sick child, the grieving widow, the brittle and arrogant power broker, and the creator God who made them all, loves them all, and grieves over their folly, their wickedness, and their sorrow—from this point of view. John wants us to see this whole story as being narrowed down and focused like a bright, blinding laser beam on the single human story of this man Jesus, the Word who became flesh—the flesh that reached out and touched the sick, the flesh that was nailed to a Roman cross.[25]

---

24. Alfayev, *Mystery of Faith*, 6
25. Wright, *Broken Signposts*, 41–42.

Chapter Ten

Abba

Knowing God Intimately

> Jesus and Paul both believed, and I believe, that in all things
> whatever the situation, however bad it may be, however
> little good is possible within it, Abba works for good.
>
> —John Cobb

> Has the thunder of "God loved the world so much" been so
> muffled by the roar of religious rhetoric that we are deaf
> to the word that God could have tender feelings for us?
>
> —Brennan Manning

My own ecumenical direction, which developed after I began to experience the deepening of God-Love (cf. John 17:20–24) in my heart, allowed me to become more open to Christians of varying doctrines and practices who came from virtually every corner of the one global church. I no longer felt my job was to correct those I disagreed with on some doctrine. (Actually, this method never worked anyway.)

Mother Maria of Normanby (1912–1977) is one example I learned from and sought to follow. Maria was born into a Methodist home in Basel, Switzerland. After leaving school she trained as a nurse, qualifying in 1935. In 1937 she was received into the Orthodox Church. After the Second World War, during which time she worked as a midwife in both Zürich and France, she embarked on six years of serious theological study. Then she went to England with the idea of entering monastic life. In 1958 she became an Orthodox nun in the Anglican Benedictine community in West Mailing. In 1965 she became an associate of the better known Sister Thekla (Marina Sharf, 1918–2011). Maria is the author of *The Psalms: An Exploratory Translation* (1973).

Mother Maria wrote a five-page preface to her psalter for daily prayer in which she takes the reader into her personal journey from studying the Psalter to singing and praying the Psalms to the moment when she received the blessing of entering into the inner life of the Psalter. This very personal approach to contemplating God's mysteries goes far beyond what language study itself can offer. It underscores that Bible study itself is not enough to touch and change the heart. We must "enter into" the truth of love. The Psalter itself has often invited Christians to "enter into" God-Love. This is one reason the daily reading and praying of the Psalms has proven so effective in forming the heart of Christians.

Sadly, Maria's life and work are not widely known in the West. Her urging to "enter into" God-Love expresses the most important conclusion I also reached through my own journey into God-Love. This also reveals the reason why various forms of academic theology miss the transforming truth of divine love. I believe my point is clear: Truth is not a system of thought. *Truth is a person.* We see the truth in the person of Christ Jesus who perfectly reveals the heart of the Father. To read Scripture well, and to pray well, we must *see* Truth in this personal way.

A Cry from the Heart of Jesus

I believe it can be said that *the most revolutionary insight* Jesus ever expressed was to call God his Abba. Jesus' understanding of Abba's love, *especially as intimate and tender affection*, clearly went beyond anything Israel had ever understood about Yahweh. Jesus' Abba *is* the God of Abraham, Moses and the prophets, but his Abba has *now* been revealed as our Father to you and me.[1]

---

1. One of the reasons for the popularity of the books of authors like Henri Nouwen, Brennan Manning, Dallas Willard, and even Richard Rohr, can be seen in the profound hunger Christians have for knowing *Abba* as intimate, tender, and compassionate love.

John B. Cobb Jr., a liberal Protestant process theologian, wrote a magnificent book in 2015—*Jesus' Abba: The God Who Has Not Failed*—in which he addressed the importance of *abba* in Scripture. Cobb says: "The prophetic God whose concerns focused on the poor and oppressed could be represented in a variety of ways." The word of the prophets was often one of judgment and mercy. Cobb concludes: "Generally, the image of God's power is of control, . . . nowhere in [the Old Testament sources] do we find this intimacy and tenderness [as] the *central theme* in understanding God. *This was the revolutionary insight of Jesus: seeing God as Abba and understanding Abba's love as intimate and tender.* Jesus' Abba is the God of the prophets qualified as love (italics mine)."[2]

What John Cobb argues for fits wonderfully with the broad, sweeping witness of the biblical texts in both the Old and New Testaments. I am persuaded that he is right in his conclusion because Jesus clearly revealed the Father as love and demonstrated this by both his words and actions. *Abba* also sums up everything about our relationship with God that we could ever desire. A modern adult catechism captures this simply and clearly: "The unfathomable depths of love between the Son and the Father are revealed in this very human word."[3]

It is evident to all who read the Gospels that Jesus is the Son of God (cf. Mark 1:1; 20:31). "A basic starting point for coming to faith in Jesus as the Son of God is Jesus' own use of this *abba* ("father") to express his relationship with God."[4] When the reader enters the world of the New Testament several changes occur that encourage a radical reorientation about God's fatherhood. This idea is no longer Israel's prerogative alone, though their experience of God was not generally conceived of in such personal terms. Now this truth belongs to all human beings. But there is more.

> [The] most radical change of all is that fatherhood is now rooted in the exceptional and unique meaning assigned to the establishment of the relation between Jesus as Son and God as Father: this novelty of meaning is now extended to other human beings, in an insistence that the latter, in imitation of Jesus, should not only refer to but actually address God as their "Father."[5]

2. Cobb Jr., *Jesus' Abba*, 11. Though Cobb embraces process theology. I am not persuaded by these views but some of his insights are nonetheless extremely valuable. His treatment of Abba is one such example.

3. *New Catechism*, 115.

4. Caba, "Abba, Father," 1.

5. Caba, "Abba, Father," 1–2.

Chiara Lubich's Journey Into Abba

Chiara Lubich, the devout Catholic from whom I first received the expression "God-Love," experienced a year of illumination that was wrapped in mystery.[6] During this year she found herself being drawn evermore deeply into the "Our Father" of the Lord's Prayer. She wrote about her relationship with the Father in a deeply personal and mystical way.

> I feel no need to explain myself, or to analyze myself, in order to present myself before You. I feel only the need to give myself wholly and entirely to You just as I am, with my sins, with the good that is in me, if there is any. And to pray to You and tell You whatever Jesus would say in my place, whatever Mary would say: And You in secret listen, understand, and accept me—I am sure—as Your daughter. Oh, who on this blessed day ever revealed to me this reality of Yours which has such an effect on my life? Certainly the Holy Spirit, to whom I offer this half hour of meditation a day. It is He who places on the edge of my lips, the word, "Abba Father." It is He who places it gently into our soul and we discover we are in our true kingdom, where we are wanted and loved just as we are.[7]

This word *abba* is Aramaic, thus it is not translated into English in most Bible versions. This word has sometimes puzzled readers. The New Testament scholar Joachim Jeremias noted that Palestinian Jews in the time of Jesus were reluctant to call God "Father."

> To the Jewish mind, it would be irreverent and therefore unthinkable to call God by this familiar word. It was something new, something unique and unheard of that Jesus dared to take this step and speak with God as a child speaks with his father, simply, intimately and securely. There is no doubt then that the *Abba* which Jesus used to address God reveals the very basis of his communion with God.[8]

So the intimate relationship we have with our Father is centered in the very relationship that Jesus had with his Father. He is *our Abba*.

---

6. Mitchell, ed., *Paradise*.
7. Mitchell, ed., *Paradise*, 77–79.
8. Jeremias, *Central Message of the New Testament*, 21.

Two Images of God in the Bible

If you have read the Bible long enough you readily recognize that there are two quite distinct images of God found in the Bible. One is *monarchical*. The other is *familial*. Running like a thread through the stories and statements of the Old Testament we see the image of a ruling, sovereign monarch. This is the image of the "King." On the other hand the New Testament gives us a more *familial* image, a God who is *our* Father (Matt 5:9). One can protest that my conclusion is simplistic, perhaps even dangerous, but reading the text for what it says, in the light of the whole, led me to this observation.

Christian understanding of God has generally focused on the Father, as Jesus taught his disciples to pray: "Our Father in heaven . . ." Paul underscores this point in many of his letters and several other New Testament authors do the same. (This emphasis does not remove the clear teaching that we must all stand before God in judgment.) I find it more than interesting that the New Testament does not picture Jesus addressing his Father as a ruler or a king. He spoke passionately and freely to his Father as his own *abba*.

Understanding the Kingdom of God

No serious student of the New Testament can doubt that the mission of Jesus was to preach and establish the kingdom of God. In Matthew (with its obvious Jewishness) this is called "the kingdom of heaven." The first declaration of Jesus in Matthew says: "Repent, for the kingdom of heaven has come near" (Matt 3:2). In Mark and Luke this same reality is called "the kingdom of God." Most scholars agree that these two expressions of the kingdom say the same thing. What is important for us to see is that Jesus freely invited *all sinners* to enter his kingdom. These kingdom texts make it clear that the purpose of Jesus' coming and dwelling among us was reconciliation, communion with God, thus our salvation. "Heaven [where God-Love reigns] has come to earth."[9] The essential condition for entering Christ's kingdom is clearly given: repent!

I believe three meanings of the kingdom can be discerned if we carefully read the Gospels. First, the kingdom is *life in God*. It means there must be a close following of God's love by following his commandments

---

9. Royster, *Kingdom of God*, 16.

and righteousness (cf. Matt 6:33; Luke 12:31). Love is so much more than a feeling! This is clearly the idea of many of Jesus' parables. Second, this kingdom comes directly to us *through God's intervention* in our world. This intervention is specifically the work of Jesus. "We begin to understand that God is establishing a society in the world separate from the world."[10] This also becomes clear in the Gospels. Jesus intended to reveal his kingdom to the world *through his disciples.* Finally, this kingdom is *present now* in those who follow Jesus. It creates a family that becomes a "separate society." This new society leads up to the second coming of Christ.[11] The kingdom is *now and not yet,* as theologians have noted. It is here among those who are in Jesus' spiritual family and it will not come in its finality until Jesus returns. Thus when we pray "your kingdom come" we are asking God to help us live this kingdom life now before Christ comes again to complete the work he began.

Doesn't this kingdom language mean we should embrace a monarchical idea of Jesus' message? This is a debated question. But from what we've seen so far it seems God's idea of the kingdom was *not* primarily that of a ruling monarch, especially when we think of a potentate who has all power and crushes all who oppose him. What if Christ's kingdom is more like a familial estate? What if his purpose is not to crush sinners but to welcome them?

In Jesus' teaching about the *basileia theou* (kingdom of God) he often said that sinners and outcasts were more likely to enter his kingdom than the religious and righteous. Why? Sinners were less likely to have success or social standing in the world. A good example of this point can be seen in how Jesus quite often spoke of wealth as an obstacle to entering the kingdom. Thus Jesus warned his disciples: "How hard it will be for those who have wealth to enter the kingdom of God!" (Mark adds: "The disciples were perplexed at these words.") But Jesus continues: "How hard it is to enter the kingdom of God! It is easier for a camel to go through the eye of a needle than for someone who is rich to enter the kingdom of God." A discussion among Jesus' disciples follows these words, in which they ask, "Then who can be saved?" Mark concludes that Jesus looked at them and said, "For mortals it is impossible, but not with God; all things are possible with God." (Mark 10:23–27). With God's love and mercy it is possible!

---

10. Royster, *Kingdom of God*, 17.

11. The most significant mistake the church made historically, and still makes in numerous ways, is to identify Christ's kingdom with the powers and governments of this world.

The point here seems to be that it is hard for adults to give up their wealth and status. To enter the kingdom requires us to strip away our social conditioning and become like little children. This is the only way to enter Christ's kingdom and to experience God's love. I honestly wonder what would happen if this became the dominant way in which we presented the gospel invitation. Some call this the way into "the upside-down kingdom." When we hear that something is "backwards," or that things have "gone upside down," we know that what's being talked about is not as it should be—it's broken, confused, and chaotic. So when we say the kingdom is upside down, it carries a connotation that paints a vivid picture.

For people of that time (and still today), this just doesn't seem right. In our world, power is often equated with prestige, wealth, and control. People strive to attain these things, believing they will bring happiness and fulfillment. But Jesus teaches us that true power and greatness come from serving others and laying down our lives for their sake. The greatest among us are those who serve. This is a familial image, not one of a powerful monarch.

What I have to wonder about is how the church moved so quickly from this obvious familial imagery and embraced the language of monarchical rule. The Greek word *pater* is our English word "father." So what happened? When the word "father" was heard in Roman and Latin contexts it sounded more like a reference to a monarch when the church gained more power in the world. But this Aramaic word *abba* has the ring of baby talk, the language of intimacy. Clearly this refers to a different kind of Father, one who reveals himself in deep tenderness. I have come to believe that a*bba* is the one word that can help draw us back into a right understanding of Christ and his kingdom (family).

Abba Texts in Context

The word *abba* is used three times in the New Testament to refer to God the Father. The first, we saw above where Jesus prays with deep passion before his impending death on the cross. He cries: "*Abba,* Father, for you all things are possible; remove this cup from me, yet not what I want but what you want" (Mark 14:36). Jesus prays in his native Aramaic and uses *abba* as an endearing title for this deeply personal relationship. Catholic scholar Eugene LaVerdiere concludes:

Jesus, the beloved Son, was being handed over by one who was not merely God, as he was for the entire universe, or Lord, as he was for his people. He was being handed over by his *personal Father*, one whom Jesus *intimately addressed as Abba*. He was being handed over so that Jesus' *Abba* might become the *Abba* of all who found life in and through Jesus (italics mine).[12]

Paul had apparently heard Mark's account of Jesus' garden prayer, perhaps from Peter. He used *abba* twice, embracing the same intimacy Jesus had with his Father by applying it to his fellow Christians. Paul's first use occurs in Romans: "For you did not receive a spirit of slavery to fall back into fear, but you received a spirit of adoption. When we cry, 'Abba! Father!'" (Rom 8:15). In Galatians Paul says virtually the same thing: "And because you are children, God has sent the Spirit of his Son into our hearts, crying, "*Abba*! Father!'" (Gal 4:6). Consider these two texts briefly.

In the first we should be reminded that Paul writes in a cultural context where slavery was real. He says Christ-followers have been delivered from bondage to sin and evil. We have been adopted. God cannot deny us. We belong to him thus we should not fear. John Chrysostom said it simply: "*Abba* Father" is here "*a special sign* of true-born children to their father."[13]

In the second Pauline text, which is in the larger context of Galatians 4:1–7, we see that in our sinful (false) self we are not heirs but minors, no better than the enslaved. We were under guardians and trustees until our Father adopted us. But now, because of the Spirit, we are God's children. We are no longer slaves but God's own children. We have inherited the whole estate and been brought into God's immediate family whereby we now call God "*Abba*." Had you lived in the first-century world you would clearly have seen how radically amazing this word is.

It strikes me as deeply significant that Paul adopted this Aramaic name for the Father that Jesus used in Mark 14: 35–36. In so doing Paul referred to our present state as that of *Abba's heirs*. Sit with this and take it in. If you belong to God you are an heir of God, a joint-heir with Christ. In the Romans 8 passage cited above we see what follows Paul's reference to *Abba*.

---

12. LaVerdiere, *Beginning of the Gospel*, 245. LaVerdiere notes that Joseph Fitzmyer, a highly regarded Catholic New Testament scholar, said: "There is no evidence in the literature of pre-Christian or first-century Palestinian Judaism that 'abba' was used in any sense as a personal address for God by an individual—and for Jesus to address God as 'abba' or 'Father' is therefore something new."

13. Royster, *St. Paul's Epistle to the Romans*, 206.

> When we cry, "*Abba*! Father!" it is that very Spirit bearing witness with our spirit that we are children of God, and if children, then heirs: heirs of God and joint heirs with Christ, if we in fact suffer with him so that we may also be glorified with him. (Rom 8:15b–16)

As noted, *abba* was not an uncommon word in Aramaic. It was the way one tenderly spoke of their father. I conclude that *abba* is more than a passing synonym for father. I believe we are warranted to ask why this word was added to these significant texts if the word "father" was enough? Abba could just as easily have been translated into English and thus the text would say "Father, Father" (Mark 14). *This would be literally true.* But the translators wished to capture the *full sense* of our relationship with God as a loving Father thus they left the word "abba" untranslated. This is how the word became known in our English Bible. (There are a few other places where Aramaic words occur in the New Testament; cf., for example Mark 5:41; 15:34). I believe Eugene Peterson was right when he used the word "Papa" for *abba*. Some still debate this conclusion. I fully embrace it.

Is Abba a Different God?

The well-known Swiss Catholic priest-theologian Hans Küng (1928–2021) concluded in his magisterial volume, *On Being a Christian,* that we are clearly warranted to say that the God who meets us in Jesus Christ is not *another* God yet he is clearly different from the God we see in the Old Testament. Küng says the God revealed in Jesus is a "better understood" God "who is also more than that omniscient being, dictating and centrally directing everything from above, who strives relentlessly to achieve his plans."[14]

The word *abba* was the word which must have struck Jesus' contemporaries "as irreverent and offensively familiar, very much as if we were to address God today as 'Dad.'" *But for Jesus familiarity does not exclude respect.* Professor Küng rightly concluded: "To address God as 'Father' is the boldest and simplest expression of that absolute trust with which we trust in God for good, for all good, with which we trust him and trust ourselves to him."[15]

---

14. Küng, *On Being a Christian*, 312.
15. Küng, *On Being a Christian*, 315.

Experiencing God's Presence

Are you convinced that God loves you like a good father who tenderly loves his own child? Scripture warrants us to say that the essence of the divine nature is compassion and the heart of God is defined by tenderness. "Because of the tender mercy of our God, the dawn from on high will break upon us to shine upon those who sit in darkness and in the shadow of death, to guide our feet into the way of peace" (Luke 1:78–79). Richard Foster captured this beautifully: "His heart is the most sensitive and tender of all. No act goes unnoticed, no matter how insignificant or small. A cup of cold water is enough to put tears in the eyes of God. Like the proud mother who is thrilled to receive a wilted bouquet of dandelions from her child so God celebrates our feeble expressions of gratitude."[16]

The popular writer Frederick Buechner often had a unique way of turning a phrase that could reach the heart. He wrote, "Repent and believe in the gospel, Jesus says. Turn around and believe the good news that we are loved is better than we ever dared hope, and that to believe in that good news, to live out of it and toward it, to be in love with that good news, is of all glad things in this world the gladdest thing of all."[17]

Most of us have had experiences that lead us to marvel and ruminate. "Music may arouse not only marvel but also other feelings that suggest the divine. It may arouse an unutterable longing or joy. Or it may evoke a deep feeling of peace and assurance." John Cobb elaborates on such a specific spiritual experience he had during World War II. He writes: "One night I knelt beside my bed to pray. Suddenly the room seemed filled by a spiritual presence that was totally accepting and loving. The joy and peace I felt was qualitatively different from any I have experienced before or since. The sense of a loving presence lasted only a few minutes, but the joyful memory remains."[18]

The Protestant Reformers, in reacting to Catholic mysticism, discouraged this type of life experience by arguing that a right relationship with God was rooted in faith alone. I believe centering on faith *alone*, at least over long periods of time, can lead us to the place where we begin to doubt God's love in unhealthy ways. What we need is an alternative, *a third way*. "This way is the way of knowing and loving abba. Abba is not just a word written about somebody, but a name spoken to somebody.

---

16. Foster, *Prayer*, 85.
17. Buechner, *Clown in the Belfry*, 171.
18. Cobb Jr., *Jesus' Abba*, 47–48.

name spoken out loud."[19]

We can experience God in this way precisely because he is love. We receive the most light on *how* God is present with us in Paul's teaching about the Christian community and the presence of the Holy Spirit. Paul saw the Spirit at work in the whole community, working internally in every believer and through the community. This work of the Holy Spirit must be experientially known. *This means God can be experienced in infinite love by the Spirit.* Bible readers know this experience of God in the New Testament as primarily the experience of grace, which is God's working in our hearts and minds.[20]

The late Brennan Manning (1934–2013), an erstwhile American Catholic priest who was widely appreciated across many Christian churches in North America, gave us some jarring and simple insights on God-Love that touched the hearts of thousands of his readers. His consistent message was centered in God as his *abba*. Manning helped me center my own life in God's acceptance of me in Christ when I began to move into the experience of the *abba's* love. Manning taught me to pray a simple prayer: "*Abba*, I belong to you!" I pray this often, especially at night before I fall asleep. Manning's fundamental conclusion fits with what we've seen: "Compassionate love is the axis of the Christian moral revolution and the only sign ever given by Jesus by which a disciple would be recognized" (John 13:34–35).[21]

Perhaps you could pause here and begin to pray this way too. Abba loves you! You do not need to do anything to earn this tender and affectionate love. In Manning's words, "Let our unworthy, ungrateful selves be loved as we are. Trust happens: You will trust him to the degree that you know you are loved by him."[22] My journey has shown me how this trust renews my spirit daily.

---

19. O'Mahony, *Abba! Father!*, 3.
20. Cobb Jr., *Jesus' Abba*, 49.
21. Manning, *Ragamuffin Gospel*, 158.
22. Manning, *Ruthless Trust*, 178. If you desire to see how to live the truth of abba then you cannot do much better than to read Manning. He is a great place to begin. Manning struggled mightily with alcoholism, and experienced some dark seasons in life, but he continued to trust abba to the very end.

Chapter Eleven

Love Takes Human Flesh

> The incarnation therefore is the place within history where we may know God in himself because, if our thinking begins with Jesus Christ as the revelation of God the Son in his unique relation with the Father and the Spirit, then we are in fact thinking from the center in God and not from a center in ourselves.
>
> —T. F. Torrance

> The Word made himself "bearer of the flesh" in order that human beings might become "bearers of the Spirit."
>
> —Olivier Clément

Jesus did not leave us written records. Furthermore, there are no Roman records of the first century that tell us anything important about Jesus. What we know about Jesus of Nazareth is due primarily to the sayings and stories that became the currency of the earliest Christians. These sayings and stories were first shared orally; then, over time, they were shaped by his apostles, written down and collected by churches. These sayings became the twenty-seven books of our New Testament. The deepest wells of Christian thought emerge in these writings. Christians believe this is a "living" tradition that has produced endless commentaries, sermons, and books. But this much everyone recognizes: The New Testament remains the primary source for what we know about Jesus. Interpreting it well requires a community, indeed a global community. This task has never been easy but it has always brought life where it has been reverently embraced. It still does.

We have a pretty clear account of this process in the Gospel of Luke (1:1–3).

> So many others have tried their hand at putting together a story of the wonderful harvest of Scripture and history that took place among us, using reports handed down by the original eyewitnesses who served this Word with their very lives. Since I have investigated all the reports in close detail, starting from the story's beginning, I decided to write it all out for you, most honorable Theophilus, so you can know beyond the shadow of a doubt the reliability of what you were taught. (MSG)

Our four Gospels—Matthew, Mark, Luke, and John—provide us with the basic story of Jesus, the story that shapes life-transforming faith. (These books are not, strictly speaking, biographies, though they contain accounts of what Jesus said and did.) Two modern scholars have accurately concluded that "For much of Church history 'Jesus' meant simply 'the one whose life, death, Resurrection, and Ascension are rendered here.'"[1]

Again we must realize that before anything was, God was and God was always love. As we've seen, love is eternal *because* God is eternal. But I submit we cannot truly see how profoundly *relational* love is without the biblical doctrine we call the incarnation. Metropolitan Anthony Bloom (a Russian Orthodox bishop) expressed this well.

> In the Incarnation we discover that God, the Holy One of Israel, the creator of the world, the beauty that surpasses all beauty, the truth and the only reality of the world—that this God chooses, *in an act of love*, so to identify himself with the destinies of humankind, so to take upon himself total and ultimate responsibility for his creative act, that all beauty of the world is called forth, while at the same time he gives the world the freedom that destroys and distorts this beauty (italics mine).[2]

---

1. Ford and Higton, eds., *Jesus*, 13.
2. *Glenstal Book of Readings for the Seasons*, 92.

The church's earliest theologians consistently said the incarnation was God's way to join himself to us. This truth prompts me to ask, "Would God have become human had the human race not fallen?" While this is a hypothetical question it remains profoundly interesting. I have come to believe that it speaks to the fullness of God's love for us. St. Isaac the Syrian reasoned that God not only took humanity as an act of restoration but as an expression of his own nature. Kallistos Ware thus concludes: "Even had there been no fall, God in his own limitless, outgoing love would still have chosen to identify himself with his creation by becoming man."[3]

Reading the Bible Well

One of the consistent problems I faced when I struggled to see the love of God as the central narrative of the Bible was how to read and understand the Bible. There is a commonly made mistake we can easily make when we first read the *entire* Bible. (I love the Bible and read it whole for the first time before my twelfth birthday.) Like most Bible readers I saw the genocide in the conquest of the Canaanites (Deut 20:16–17; 1 Sam 15:2–3) as deeply problematic. I also saw how Jesus plainly taught us to love our enemies (Matt 5–7). *It seemed apparent that something changed.* I have read a considerable number of articles and books about how these texts can be made harmonious. I now find most of these efforts at interpretation beg the real question we naturally have about these ancient stories. Therefore, I have to agree with Brian Zahnd:

> What has changed is not God but the degree to which humanity has attained an understanding of the true nature of God. The Bible is not a perfect revelation of God; Jesus is. Jesus is the only perfect theology. Perfect theology is not a system of theology, perfect theology is a person. Perfect theology is not found in abstract thought; perfect theology is found in the Incarnation.[4]

Some readers get hung up on this insight about how to correctly read the Bible. Sadly, they hear me saying that the Bible is *filled* with errors. But this is not my point. The Old Testament is the story of how Israel came to know God. It prepares the way for the Jewish Messiah. (It often shows us how *not* to live!) Furthermore, Joshua, the son of Nun, does not give us the full revelation of God. The greater Joshua, Jesus of Nazareth,

---

3. Ware, *Orthodox Way*, 70.
4. Zahnd, *Sinners in the Hands of a Loving God*, 31.

does. Joshua and David were deeply flawed men. Jesus "is the reflection of God's glory and the exact imprint of God's very being" (Heb 1:3). The difference here is striking and quite clear.

Tragically, the Scriptures have been used to justify slaughter, race-based slavery, male dominance, getting personal revenge, embracing a nation's pursuit of control over other nations and peoples, and a host of other actions supported by the selective citation of Old Testament stories as normative for Christians today. My evangelical background was filled with such problems, especially in how it understood the patriarchal idea of women submitting to men. This has now led to the promotion of the idea that America is a chosen "Christian nation," something never advanced in the Bible itself. Not only has this been a historic tragedy but it has been clearly revealed that this American god is not the God and Father of our Lord Jesus Christ! This god is an idol for far too many modern Christians.

The Relational God

I have already addressed a key idea about God and now must again show why this matters to how we understand the biblical story of love. We've seen that God established a loving relationship with his creatures. This was especially true with Israel in the Old Testament. Terence E. Fretheim noted that the biblical metaphors for God "have relatedness at their core." And, "These kinds of relational images for God reveal a God who has entered deeply into the life of the world and is present and active in the common life of individuals and communities."[5] You will never read the Bible well until you see his point.

The Bible also makes it abundantly clear that "The human being, with all the capacities for relationship . . . [is] the most appropriate image of God in the life of the world. The relational God of the Old Testament is not first and foremost the God of Israel, but the God of the whole world. God was in a relationship with the world before there ever was an Israel. God's relationship with Israel must be understood as a subset, albeit a deeply significant one, within the more inclusive and comprehensive divine-world relationship (Gen. 12:3)."[6]

---

5. Fretheim, *God So Enters Into Relationships That . . . A Biblical View*, 23.
6. Fretheim, *God So Enters Into Relationships That . . . A Biblical View*, 23.

The Mysterium Christi

There is a story in English literature of a little boy hearing about the crucifixion of Jesus and responding to the story by saying, "If God had been there, he would not have let them do it." *Here we see the real mystery of the incarnation.* Why? The whole of the Christian tradition rests on this truth: *God was there! God was in Christ dying for us because of infinite love.*

John S. Whale (1896–1996), a Scottish Congregational minister and theologian, wrote: "It is a matter of historic experience that out of this lowest depth to which the race of men could go down, God made his highest revelation. God's mind and act are shown forth out of the very stuff of events which supremely illustrate man's mind and act. This is the Lord's doing and it is marvelous in our eyes."[7]

The question that must always be before us if we are to truly know God's love is this: Who is Jesus Christ?[8] The answers that have been offered are too numerous to enumerate them here. However, scholars and non-scholars alike have often missed the most basic answer to this question. The Gospels actually provide us with two clear answers.

Jesus Was Human

Jesus Christ was a man, in the full psychological and physical sense. He truly and fully shared in all the conditions of our humanity. He was "flesh of our flesh." He was *not* a phantom, archangel, or demigod. He did not merely play the role of a human person. Hebrews 2:14–18 makes this exceptionally clear. To really know Jesus is to believe that he is "God-with-us." He is not just a role model or a good teacher. Jesus is exactly like us; yet he completely surpasses any of us. But before we proceed we need to understand that Jesus wasn't half God and half human; he was fully God and fully human. This is what Christians believed and confessed in the Creed.

---

7. Whale, *Christian Doctrine*, 98.

8. Christ comes from the Greek word χριστός (chrīstós), meaning "anointed one." In the Greek Septuagint, χριστός was a semantic loan word used to translate the Hebrew word for the Messiah. Thus "Jesus Christ," in the New Testament refers to Jesus as the "anointed one," or the Messiah.

Jesus Was God

The second distinctive fact about Jesus revealed in the Gospels is this: Jesus was God in human flesh. In Jesus Christ we not only meet a *real man* but we see *the living God*.

> [Jesus] is God himself, personally present and redeemingly active, who comes to meet [humanity] in this Jesus of Nazareth. Jesus is more than a religious genius . . . The Jesus, who merely illustrates general religious truths (so called), is neither the Jesus of the Gospels nor the living Lord of the apostles and martyrs. . . . God's presence and his very Self were made manifest in the words and works of this man.[9]

In these two stupendous claims we can affirm that Jesus was fully and completely man and fully and completely God. Everything Christians believe about God rests on these two profound truths. The theology of this has been called "the two natures of Christ." These two natures, one human and one divine, are not mixed or mingled but make a completely new nature. These ideas are distinct and essential if we are to understand Jesus.

Jesus Fully Reveals God's Grace

The grace of God is a constant theme in Scripture, whether the word is used or not. Grace tells us a great deal about who God is. As we have seen, God's nature is defined by self-giving love. Grace is the loving kindness of God towards those he loves. "This is seen in his relentless mercy towards his errant children and his unfailing love in the face of the faithless and the loveless behavior of those whom he has created. In this sense, the word 'grace' describes what God is like, and what God is like is self-giving love."[10]

The grace of God describes what we can ultimately say about God's gift of Jesus for us and our salvation. John 3:16 underscores this grace perfectly. But to say that grace tells us about who God is in love does not mean that grace is a divine attribute. I maintain that grace and love are not attributes but something intensely personal and active. "Love is

---

9. Whale, *Christian Doctrine*, 101.
10. Groves, *Grace*, 3.

what God is, something active and dynamic, and so grace is not simply a characteristic."[11]

The Australian Redemptorist priest Anthony J. Kelly perfectly expresses how God's grace is rooted in divine love: "We affirm 'God is Love' because in Christ God is self-expressed. In him all humanity finds its fulfillment and ultimate blessing in God. The reality of this love means that Jesus is neither a Divine Person hiding behind a human face nor a human person adopted into a divine sphere."[12] Christian faith is not based on a principle of thought or even action, or on inspired writings, so much as on this one unique person. "Christian faith means living a relationship with this God-given, humanly named Other."[13]

The Struggle

The early church developed this thinking about Jesus by deeply grappling with texts such as John 1:1–18. There are five verses in this prologue that stand out regarding the person of Jesus. First, "In the beginning was the Word, and the Word was with God, and the Word *was* God. He was *in the beginning* with God. All things came into being *through* him, and *without* him not one thing came into being." (verses 1–3). The Logos (Word) was "with" God and the Logos was "God." John says, "And the Word *became* flesh and lived among us, and we have seen his glory, the glory as of a father's only son, full of grace and truth" (verse 14). Finally, we see that the Son is *not* the Father but rather he made the Father known because Jesus *is* God. No one has ever seen God. It is the only Son, *himself God*, who is close to the Father's heart, who has *made him known* (verse 18). John's clear affirmations address almost all of the false ideas about Jesus that surfaced in the early church and have continued down to this day.

In texts like these, joined with the various confessions of those who encountered Jesus, we see how a nascent first-century movement within Judaism *became* Christianity. As the number of gentile believers in Jesus grew, especially after the destruction of the Jewish temple (70 CE), this little flock of Jesus' followers took on a unique identity all its own. This identity was never *without* Jewish roots. Indeed, any attempt to understand Jesus without his Jewish background will always get things wrong.

---

11. Groves, *Grace*, 3.
12. Kelly, *God Is Love*, 33.
13. Kelly, *God Is Love*, 34.

(A careful study of these accounts shows they did absolutely nothing to remove this essential background of the Jewishness of Jesus.) Jesus quoted the Old Testament Scriptures as the basis for his own words and actions. His followers sought to continue their reflection on how the life of this Jewish Messiah fit within the wider world of Judaism. They consistently used the Old Testament Scriptures to do this.

It is widely recognized that the background of earliest Christian thought about the incarnation happened within a constant struggle between two primary influences: the Jewish background of Jesus and the Greco-Roman culture that shaped a growing understanding of the gospel. "In both cases, the claims Christians made about the man Jesus of Nazareth were central to the sense of their own identity which they developed."[14]

Some wonder if we can really have a distinct theology of Jesus (Christology). After living with the *mysterium Christi* for a lifetime I am persuaded the testimony we see on virtually every page of the New Testament was *explicitly recognized* during the first few centuries of the church. "The Christological debates of nineteen centuries are a monument to the uniqueness of him whom Christians know as the Incarnate Son of God. The very existence of a Christology is profoundly significant. There is no Mohammedology so far as I know. Nor have I ever heard of a Socratology."[15]

How Then Do We Resolve the Tensions of This Doctrine?

There is an obvious tension in what we see in the New Testament regarding Jesus. So I think we are warranted to ask: How do we resolve it? The technical formula agreed upon in the fifth century chose the phrase "two natures in one person." This was a Greek way of saying that the incarnate Christ transcended the power of all logic to discover a *synthesis*. "The unending attempt to correlate the human and the divine in Jesus Christ is a monument to this mystery."[16] *If you deny the mystery of Christ's person you will not have the Christ of the Gospels.* But if you try to explain it, so as to settle all the intellectual debates, you will quite likely get lost in the weeds

---

14. Ford and Higton, eds., *Jesus*, 60.
15. Whale, *Christian Doctrine*, 109.
16. Whale, *Christian Doctrine*, 110.

and maybe even lose the Jesus who said: "I am the way and the truth and the life. No one comes to the Father except through me" (John 14:6).

The Hunger We Share

I am persuaded we all share a universal hunger to love and be loved. We form simple friendships as children. If we are emotionally healthy this hunger for love will mature as we form different types of friendships in adolescence and later as adults. Our friendships will change and grow, or they will fade away. Many of us seek a lifelong companion, who will be our dearest friend, so we get married. The truth is obvious—we pursue friendships because we were made this way. Eventually we learn that no person we've ever met is completely open and totally reliable. I am persuaded that the fulfillment we all seek in these relationships is to be finally found in the love of God. More specifically this love is found in Jesus. Does this mean we seek to experience the love of God and neglect our everyday responsibilities? The Ignatian principle has proven helpful to me when it says we "find God in all things" while we avoid "finding gods among things." When we give ourselves to the reality of God-Love all other licit loves fall into place by ordering our love for God.

Fr. George Maloney (1924–2005), who wrote over eighty books, gave his life to teaching this truth about Jesus and love. I call his insight the "friendship factor."

> We are this way by God's plan, hungering to find someone else to always be open, vulnerable, totally available as a loving presence, eager to share ourselves on a certain degree of equality on the greatest levels of human awareness on body, soul and spirit levels. We ever so slowly learn through our stubborn resistance to the truth that will call us into our unique and beautiful personhood except that we and our loved ones are ready to die to any self-centeredness and be ready at all times in all circumstances to sacrifice oneself for the happiness of the other.[17]

Because of the incarnation we can have a deep relationship with the person of Jesus and truly love other human beings. But why? God made himself completely available to us in human flesh because he is love. For love he sent his Son for us and our salvation.

---

17. Maloney, *God's Community of Love*, 23.

I am also persuaded that the mystery of Christ is not something God hid from us but rather something we do not understand until the Spirit reveals Christ to us. A Seventh-day Adventist author has cogently written that on the basis of Philippians 2:5–11 we can say God took "seven downward steps" in order to reach us. "Here is the consummate revelation of the true heart and mind of God. Here is how utterly selfless and other-centered is his love. No playacting! God the Son literally did not regard His position of equality with God the Father to be greater than our salvation."[18]

The Cloud and the Servant

In chapter 1 we saw that on the Mount of Transfiguration there was light and a cloud that surrounded Jesus and his three disciples. This image is a vivid reminder of the *mystery of our faith*. When Jesus was baptized he heard a voice from heaven say: "This is my Son, the Beloved, with whom I am well pleased" (Matt 3:17). This "well pleased" of the Father is what was seen on the mountain. In Matthew 12:15–21 we read yet another amazing account of the Father being well pleased with his Son.

Jesus is God's chosen servant, chosen to carry out his Father's purpose to save and heal both Jew and gentile alike. It is this message of burning love from heaven that the three disciples heard and saw on the Mount of Transfiguration (Matt 17:1–8). But, and this is important to see, this message could not be fully understood until *after* Jesus had risen and ascended.

These various passages reveal that the mystery of God's nature is *love revealed, a love that is a communion of persons*. Jesus is loved by his Father and his Father loves him as his *only begotten* Son. But what becomes even more clear when you read these texts carefully is this: we can never *comprehend* God's *inner life*.

> In our poverty and utter creatureliness, even in our sinfulness and alienation from the Father, we realize, that to know God intimately and to dare even to imagine living a life of God's intimate, self-sacrificing love in total availability and mutuality in the greatest intimate union as children, made by God's grace participators in his own divine nature (2 Pt. 1:4), lies beyond our own power.[19]

18. Gibson, *An Endless Falling in Love*, 83.
19. Maloney, *God's Community of Love*, 25.

George Maloney had a unique way of making the complex quite clear. He said the more we grow spiritually the more we realize that *God must make himself known to us*. We do not reach God by climbing religious ladders. We do not earn his love. We know his love only by grace. "We can only humbly wait in the desert of our nothingness, hoping to receive God as he wishes to make himself known to us. With the humility of children we seek entrance into the heart of God as he communicates himself to his Word through his Spirit of love."[20]

I am fully persuaded that the teaching of Jesus on this subject is plain—he came to bring us into *intimate communion* with himself and the Father through divine love. This is so much more than knowledge or communication of religious information. This is the deepest mystery of personal communion.

Can the Incomprehensible Mystery Become Comprehensible?

The famous Catholic philosopher Étienne Gilson grasped this mystery. "Any God who is not inaccessible, man can dispense with. It is the God who is by his nature inaccessible whom man cannot do without."[21] Ignatius of Antioch said God manifests himself *through* his Word: "There is one God, who manifested himself through Jesus Christ his Son, who is his Word proceeding from silence."[22]

Thus Jesus is *the human face of God*. In the incarnate Christ we experience God communicating through the medium of human experience. The famous Scottish theologian John Macquarie (1919–2007), expressed this profoundly and simply by writing: "To say that Christ is the human face of God is, of course, to assert nothing less than that he is God, and at an early stage in the history of the church Christians realized that one cannot worship Christ or attach ultimacy to his teachings or make for him the claims that Christians do make, if he is anything less than God."[23]

This mystery of godliness is the true power that resides in God's holy character. This mystery, as we've now seen in several ways, *is* the

---

20. Maloney, *God's Community of Love*, 25.
21. Gilson, *Mystical Theology of St. Bernard*, 120.
22. Cited by Maloney, *God's Community of Love*, 27.
23. From *The Humility of God*, quoted in *The Glenstal Book of Readings for the Seasons*, 204. John Macquarie was one of the best twentieth-century theologians who developed a divine love theology.

very character of God. Therefore this mystery is self-sacrificing love. One author has rightly said, "God would rather make himself nothing than allow you and me to be eternally lost."[24]

Everything Comes from the Father

Jesus is the Word made flesh, the one who receives all power from his Father. He can do nothing of himself. Thus what he receives he gives. He receives his Abba's love and he shares this same intimate, tender love with us.

Jesus said: "[T]he word that you hear is not mine but is from the Father who sent me" (John 14:24). This is why the church said of Jesus that he is "light from light, true God from true God." This mystery is so great that it can never be fully grasped by our minds alone. The perfect God of love gives himself for us in the Son who is "the way, the truth and the life" (John 14:26).

You will have noticed by now how prominently this truth can be seen in the Gospel of John. I observed over the years, especially after preaching verse-by-verse through the Fourth Gospel, that this truth is at one and the same time clear, yet it is always utterly profound. It nourishes the heart while at the same time it baffles our intellect. *Jesus is the light of the world and his light shines within our hearts to show us his Father.* He is the *life* of the world thus he sustains and re-creates all that is good in life. He is our *source* and *sustainer* and his energy re-creates all that is good. His *caring* is the source of true good in the world. And his *power transforms*.[25] "He is the concentrated energy, the explosive force which breaks-up, in order to make new."[26]

What Happened When Jesus Came?

Professor Norman Wirzba profoundly expresses what is central in seeing how the incarnation *means* God-Love.

> When the world is in trouble and life is being degraded or destroyed, the love of God goes to work in acts of healing. It

---

24. Gibson, *An Endless Falling in Love*, 87.

25. The Greek word for power is *dunamis*, e.g. used for power, miraculous works, and specific spiritual gifts manifest in individual believers through the Holy Spirit's anointing.

26. Clasper, *Eastern Paths and the Christian Way*, 71.

responds by exposing and countering the counterfeit, corrupted forms of love that get in the way of genuine life. Love's desire, always, is that all creatures be well and attain the fullness of their being, which is why when creatures are wounded, love gets busy to bring about healing.[27]

I like this phrase, "Love goes to work." Indeed, it always does. Love came down and love went to work! There are far more dimensions to the work of God-Love than we can explore in a relatively short book but suffice it to say that the love of Jesus heals, unites, and gives us the insight to think rightly about ourselves. Love creates and builds community. If I have learned anything in living with chronic weakness for nearly three decades it is this: forgiveness is intimately connected to healing and love is the power that makes this forgiveness and healing actually happen. "The difference between sickness and health depends on the strength of the love that is there at work. As the power of love increases, so too does the capacity to live."[28] I do not merely write this as a theory. I have experienced it in the deepest recesses of my own heart.

The prophet Isaiah, centuries before the coming of Jesus, wrote: "The people who walked in darkness have seen a great light; those who lived in the land of deep darkness—on them light has shined" (9:2). The Gospels make it abundantly plain that this "great light" was the Messiah Jesus. This is the same light Moses saw in the burning bush as well as that which was revealed to the three disciples on the Mount of Transfiguration. After Jesus was raised and ascended they "saw" this light clearly.

Love Makes God Who God Is

So we can see that Jesus is both God and man, fully entering into our human pain. Yet Jesus was singularly uninterested in lofty ideas or great projects. *He was greatly interested in transforming life from deep within.* Why? Jesus is God living out our deepest questions and most intense struggles. Jesus is God creating new life in all our brokenness. Jesus is God embracing us as his intimate friends.

Orthodox theologian John Zizioulas (1931–2023) rightly concluded: "Love, as God's mode of existence, 'hypostatizes' God (i.e., it makes

---

27. Wirzba, *Way of Love*, 145.
28. Wirzba, *Way of Love*, 147.

God's person) . . . constitutes His being."[29] Thus love is not a quality or property, or even a characteristic of a simple divine substance but God-Love is "that which makes God who God is, the one God" who is three persons in perfect communion.[30] This is where we turn next to consider the Trinity as love.

This really is the transforming power of love revealed in Jesus Christ who is himself incarnate love.

---

29. Zizioulas, *Being as Communion*, 46. This is one of the finest treatments of the nature of God as love that I have read.

30. Zizioulas, *Being as Communion*, 46.

Chapter Twelve

The Trinity of Love

Christians adore the divine community of Father, Son and Spirit. God is not solitary, but rather an unimaginable and unbounded Love-life of interpersonal giving and receiving.

—Anthony J. Kelly

God wishes not just to communicate ideas about his divine nature to us, but to be in intimate *communion*, ecstatic union, with each of us.

—George Maloney

All shall be well, and all shall be well, and all manner of thing shall be well.

—Julian of Norwich

What we clearly know about God is not what we are clever enough to figure out. What we truly know *is* eternal life. John makes this abundantly clear: "Father, the hour has come; glorify your Son so that the Son may glorify you, since you have given him authority over all people, to give eternal life to all whom you have given him. And *this is eternal life, that they may know you*, the only true God, and Jesus Christ, whom you have sent" (John 17:1–3). This eternal life is not a quantity of life and clearly not limited to life after death. It is the quality of life that God gives right now and it continues forever. Simply put, it is a life of God-Love. Why? Because God's nature is generous, overflowing, self-giving love. When all our human thoughts are set aside we begin to see what will finally remain is love because God remains, and God is love. Evelyn Underhill put this well: "We believe that the tendency to give, to share, to cherish, is all the mainspring of the universe, the ultimate cause of all that is, and [this] reveals the Nature of God."[1]

Hans Urs von Balthasar, perhaps more than any other modern theologian, developed a careful, consistent theology of God's love. He concluded that love is "the quintessence of all reality." He based this staggering claim upon the truth that "God is love." If God is love then this "sentence supports the whole Christian message."[2] Balthasar constantly argued that Christians often treat God's love as a truth but only in an *abstract* sense. (As you've seen this is what I did for several decades.) Balthasar reasons that for many of us love is not a truth that we allow to impact our daily lives. This is the very thesis of my book. *We must allow God's love to radically impact our lives every day, all the time.*

So what has the Trinity to do with this fire of transforming love?

God Is One and God Is Trinity

There can be no serious doubt that both Eastern and Western Christians believed that God is One. Yet the church catholic believed the Creator God was revealed in three distinct persons—the Father, the Son, and the Holy Spirit. Thus, the Father, the Son, and the Holy Spirit are God; not *three* gods. While it has become popular, as it was in earlier centuries, to cast doubt upon this cardinal truth, I maintain that the Trinity remains the primary theological bulwark for understanding the nature of God as love. History shows that the confession of God as the Father, the Son, and the Holy Spirit is the clearest expression of *personal love we have*. But why? God's love is always the love of *three persons who eternally love one*

---

1. Underhill, Barkway, and Menzies, eds., *Anthology of the Love of God*, 42–43.
2. Clements, *Meaning of the World is Love*, 23.

another. This truth was passed down by the first Christian theologians because they articulated what they encountered in the words of the apostles.[3]

Therefore, we are warranted to say that God is Trinity precisely because God is love. But why? God cannot love, and be loved, unless the Trinity is true. God-Love necessarily existed before creation if God is eternal love.

This is one reason why the church confessed the Holy Spirit as God, because of his infinite power of loving. He has been rightly called "the love bond" of the Trinity.

But Is the Trinity Biblical?

The most common objection to the doctrine of the Trinity, at least among those who read the Bible, goes something like this—there is no *clear single* reference to the Trinity in the Bible. I am still amazed when I hear this objection. It flows out of a prooftexting approach we've already seen. Where then is a verse that clearly says God *is* Trinity? (There are several texts that name the Father, the Son, and the Holy Spirit; cf. Matt 28:19, Gal 4:6.)

For this, and several other reasons, some of our best religious friends question the doctrine of the Trinity. For them it is an impossible contradiction. Both Muslims and Jews, who are people of the book, wonder if Christians are really monotheists. It sounds to them like we believe in three gods. When Christians say they believe in one God, but also in the Father who is God, the Son who is God, and the Spirit who is God, it sounds terribly confusing. The fact that this doctrine is not spelled out in a single New Testament text should give us a great measure of humility. The popular Methodist pastor Adam Hamilton expresses this in a simple way: "My own conviction is that the three pounds of gray matter we call the brain is not up to the task of fully comprehending the nature of God."[4]

One alternative to the Trinity stressed that God was not only one but singular, which itself is deeply rooted in another Greek idea. Another option was offered by the famous Marcion (85–160), who in effect said there are *several* gods. Marcion taught that the God of the Old Testament,

---

3. I am fully aware of the ways some deny the Trinity. It is not my purpose here to defend this teaching. No church father taught that this doctrine was open to serious doubt. To argue that because the political aspects of this debate had a significant role in its written formulation in the creed does not negate the simple fact that all Christians believed it to be true based upon their careful reading of the New Testament.

4. Hamilton, *Creed*, 91.

the Creator, was *inferior* to Christ. (Sadly, this is how many still read the Old Testament.)

Another more subtle alternative to the Trinity said that God was one person in three *forms*. Still another alternative said God the Father is a little *more divine* than Jesus the Son. The first idea is called *modalism*, in which the Father, Son, and Holy Spirit are mere *manifestations* (or modes) of God. The second major error was called *subordinationism*. This idea said the Son was *not fully God* as the Father is fully God. The Son and the Spirit are *completely subordinate*. I agree with the creeds that the Trinity is essential to Christian faith. (Note how the Apostles' Creed has three stanzas, one dealing with each person in the Trinity.)

Let's be honest. No one has ever fully comprehended the doctrine of the Trinity. We use technical terms, as well as analogies, charts, and icons, but this truth remains a paradox. The work of our best theologians in explaining this might be compared to how physicists try to explain something that most intelligent people struggle to comprehend. "How do you explain a world that works at the subatomic level?" Personally, I have no idea but I accept that the world operates in this way.

But what has the Trinity *specifically* to do with the deep mystery we call divine love?

The Love That Is in Christ

A straightforward reading of Paul's epistles underscores an important theological truth that supports the Trinity. Here is just one example: "But now *in Christ Jesus* you who once were far away have been brought near by the blood of Christ" (Eph 2:13). What does Paul mean when he speaks of our being *in Christ Jesus*? There can be no reasonable doubt he is saying we *participate* in Christ; that is, in his life, in his death, and in his resurrection and ascension. This has been called the doctrine of union with Christ. But what does this *union* mean?

To answer we turn again to the Gospel of John. Consider John 17 where Jesus prays to his Father before he faces his horrible death. He finds comfort by recalling the love that he shared with his Father "before the world existed" (17:5, cf. verses 24, 26). His prayer reaches a profound crescendo in verse 21 where he prays: "As you, Father, are *in me* and I am *in you*, may they also be *in us*." Addressing his Father, he prays: "I made your name known to them, and I will make it known, so that the love with which you loved me may be *in them*, and I *in them*" (verse 26, italics added). This idea is clearly *participation*. Jesus introduces us to the love of his Father, which he knew before the world was created.

We are brought face to face here with the profound *interrelationship* between the Father, the Son, and the Holy Spirit. The Christian believer participates in this eternal relational love. The believer's "indwelling [within] the life of God is the heart and soul of John's understanding of salvation," in that "every believer's inclusion within the exchange of divine life and love between the Father and Son is the essence . . . of [John's] message about eternal life."[5]

This relationship of participation in the very life of God is clearly mysterious. For years I tried to understand it with my mind. I wanted to understand how I died with Christ and how I could live by his presence working in me. The more I read the more I did not understand. Frankly, it all seemed rather bizarre. It just made no sense. Now I have embraced this truth through faith in the Trinity. This has led me to pray daily that I will be transformed by it. This truth of my participation in Christ is clearly established by the ministry of all three persons of the Trinity. No other biblical doctrine makes this remotely understandable.

God Is Love in Himself

In loving us God established a holy *communion* of love. Cardinal Walter Kasper said the scriptural announcement that "God is love" is an ontological announcement because it reveals the being most proper to God.[6] Only because God is love can God reveal himself and share himself with us as love. Think about it. If God is not love he cannot share his life of love with us. *But God is love and his love is a trinitarian relationship of persons*. Thus we share in God's love *because* in the Son we have come to know and participate in the love of the Trinity. The Trinity is the divine reality which underscores *how* God can really be *eternal* love. "From all eternity, in his unique essence—which is love—he exists trinitarianly, that is differentiating (because he is love and a total gift of himself) into

---

5. David Cramp, "Re-Examining the Johannine Trinity," cited in Wessling, *Love Divine*, 221.

6. Ontology refers to what proceeds from God to reality. Rolf A. Jacobson says, "You can sum up ontology by the commonsense observation 'If it ain't one thing, it's another'" (*Crazy Talk*, 219). A simple theological example is the difference between God and a human being. Ontology reflects on this difference.

the persons of the Father, the Son and the Spirit, therefore in an 'affable plural,' which at the same time is perfect unity."[7]

The words of St. Augustine give us a further glimpse into a classic treatment of the Trinity and God's love.

> In truth you see the Trinity if you see love. There are three: the lover, the loved and love. And not more than three: one who loves the one who comes from him, one who loves the one from whom he came, and love itself. . . . And if this doesn't mean anything, in what way can it be that God is love? And if there is no substance here, in what way is God substance?[8]

It will be a real grace to you to read St. Augustine's idea several times.

Modern Distortions

The famous American Protestant theologian H. Richard Niebuhr rightly observed that the demise of Trinitarian faith is always followed by varieties of unitarianism.[9] American Christian history profoundly demonstrates his point. So-called cults abound in America's individualistic soil. So-called revivals often fostered these nonorthodox ideas. The denial of the essential truth about who God is, the one who is love in Trinity, has always led to errors and extremes. I am fully persuaded that such distortions break the bonds of God-Love revealed to us in the Scripture. Here are several such distortions.

First, there is the distortion seen in a form of American unitarianism that stresses the Creator to the exclusion of the Son. This leads many to think of the god in the US Constitution—thus the god of unalienable rights—as the one who has guided America's destiny and greatness. We have seen a huge revival of this kind of thinking by confusing the triune God of the Bible with the hero god of Americanism.

Second, there is a popular modern distortion that elevates Jesus the redeemer to "Jesus *my* personal Savior." This is an error I learned in my evangelical background. At the popular level this can be seen on the bumper sticker: "Honk if you love Jesus!" Salvation is defined almost exclusively in terms of *my* personal welfare. One of the most serious errors of this thinking leads to what one calls "Jesusolatry." A focus on Jesus

---

7. Cerini, *God Who Is Love*, citing Walter Kasper, 41.
8. Augustine, *Trinitate*, quoted by Marisa Cerini, *God Who Is Love*, 76.
9. Migliore, *Faith Seeking Understanding*, 75.

alone elevates a sentimental attachment to Christ and misses the deep concern of the triune God for justice and care for the earth. This distortion avoids getting messy with the things of earth since all else will "grow strangely dim" when you turn your eyes upon Jesus. (More than a few imbalanced ideas are expressed in our hymns and popular praise songs.)

Third, there is a distortion that comes when the experience of the Holy Spirit becomes separated from the Father and the Son. There is often too little effort made to "test the spirits" to see if the Spirit of God's Christ has been kept central. J. I. Packer once told me what I have never forgotten—we must understand that the Spirit was given to shine light upon Jesus! Love is revealed in Jesus but the Spirit truly makes this love ours. The loss of this proper emphasis on the Spirit has been a real problem in Western Christianity. The "solution to the problem is not more revelry in intense religious experience."[10] The experience of the Holy Spirit must always be situated in the experience of the triune God.

The Grammar of the Trinity

From the earliest Christian centuries theologians have rightly acknowledged that the Trinity is the greatest mystery of our faith. But they have never ignored it. *Every creed, every liturgy, and every written orthodox theology has consistently and faithfully maintained this mystery.* Our best hymns express it. St. Augustine probably spent more time wrestling with this than any other early theologian. He understood this well when he wrote: "If you comprehend something, it is not God."[11]

The grammar of the Trinity is sometimes complicated but it is always full of life-giving meaning. Take for example the almost exclusive imagery of God expressed in masculine terms in the Bible. Some contemporary theologians suggest we do away with gender-specific language altogether. They suggest we use impersonal pronouns and metaphors for God. I rather prefer to use the various biblical pronouns with far more care, e.g., we can positively speak of the Spirit, for example, as feminine. "[We can lose] the biblical truth of addressing God not only as a father who cares for and protects his chosen people (1 Chron. 22:10; Ps. 103:13; Matt. 6:6–9) but also as a mother who gives birth to, feeds, and comforts her children (Isa. 49:15; 66:12–13)." Whatever we say and do we cannot

---

10. Migliore, *Faith Seeking Understanding*, 76.
11. Cited by Migliore, *Faith Seeking Understanding*, 77.

afford to lose this emphasis on God as personal. A modern confession of faith stresses what Scripture means when it says God is "like a mother who will not forsake her nursing child, like a father who runs to welcome the prodigal home."[12] That is clearly a sound biblical emphasis.

In the work of creation, reconciliation, and redemption God never acts "out of character."[13] This is also what the Trinity means. God's character is a triune fellowship of love grounded in the love bond of three persons in eternal unity. If God's work in redemption is to draw us back into the fullness of divine love then this love is deeply grounded in the Father, the Son, and the Holy Spirit.

A Unity of Persons as the Bond of Love

When what I've said is kept in mind we can begin to see that the unity of the triune God is always *a unity of persons in the bond of love*. Sharing a common essence, the Father, the Son, and the Spirit are *differentiated* by their relationships with each other, thus the indwelling between the persons is always *mutual*. Again this is great mystery and this mystery profoundly nourishes the soul of both the individual and the church.[14]

I have referred to God as *relational* several times. To confess that God is triune means God exists in a communion of relationships that is far deeper than the kind of partnerships we commonly know. (The Bible uses marriage to tell us something important about this truth. As we become one in the union of marriage so we become one with the persons of the Trinity in our salvation.) *The essence of the Trinity is deeply relational oneness in love.* God's unity is not abstract sameness but a rich and dynamic unity of plentitude. Thus the "mutual indwelling" of the persons captures the idea behind the important Greek word *perichoresis*. This unique word literally means "interpenetration." The word was first adopted by theologians of the church to describe the mutual indwelling

---

12. Migliore, *Faith Seeking Understanding*, 78. This wording, which for me is clearly biblical, is found in the *Brief Statement of Faith* adopted by the Presbyterian Church USA.

13. Migliore, *Faith Seeking Understanding*, 79.

14. Several important twentieth-century theologians, such as Karl Barth and Karl Rahner, expressed reticence about speaking of God as a "person." They saw this primarily as philosophical language which constituted autonomous existence. I rather see the sharing of life between the Father, the Son, and the Spirit as a differentiation that supports the mutual giving and receiving between the persons we see in the language of the New Testament.

of the divine and human natures in the incarnate Word. It suggests an *intimacy* beyond any relationship known to human persons. It has been noted that it has the connotations of "a dance" of three persons in perfect love and harmony. In a more active sense *perichoresis* is the idea of God moving in and through someone or something. Moltmann suggested that the *perichoresis* is like a swirling or a dance. (Don't tell some Christians that the Trinity might be understood as a dance of eternal love!)

Most discussions of the Trinity use models to explain this unity. (Many of the popular models I was taught as a child were moralistic and proved quite unhelpful.) One good model is the *psychological analogy* of persons. In this model the three persons are differentiated but inseparable activities of the self. "To be a person is to be a self-conscious subject possessing the intertwined faculties of memory, understanding, and will."[15]

A second model has been called the *social analogy*. This analogy takes the human experience of life as our best clue to what the relationship of the three persons means. A favorite triad is lover, beloved, and mutual love. Western theology has traditionally given preference to the psychological model while a growing number of modern theologians have leaned more heavily on the social analogy, which is closer to the tradition of Orthodoxy.

While a case can be made for both of these analogies they clearly have been misused. We should note that the church has never confessed either one of them as the *right one*. I am persuaded they both will help us to better understand divine love. But why? They both major on this central fact—the doctrine of the Trinity means *relationships*. *Thus we can and should say that the Father is love, the Son is love, and the Spirit is love.*

If God is love we should conclude that Jesus demonstrates divine love in a human and profoundly relational way. Remember, "The Word became flesh and lived among us, and we have seen his glory, the glory as of a father's only son, full of grace and truth" (John 1:14). Christ is the eternal God who created all things and redeems fallen persons. But how does this relate to Trinity? "The whole of humanity therefore—and in humanity the cosmos—is eternally present in the Word in the form of a plan, created through him and re-created by means of his redemptive incarnation, will come 'together under Christ, as head' (cf. Eph. 1:10),

---

15. Migliore, *Faith Seeking Understanding*, 81.

and will be definitively assumed into the eternal act of the generation of the Son by the Father, in the heart of the Trinity."[16]

Through the loving oneness of the Father and the Son, the Spirit of God *expresses* his deepest longing for us. Pope John Paul II clearly captured this idea when he said: "The Holy Spirit [is] the love of the Father and of the Son." But was he right to put the work of the Spirit in this way? This attribution—love—given to the Holy Spirit as his own name, is constant throughout the fathers and doctors of the church, while it still affirms that "love is the very essence of God therefore common to all three of the divine persons."[17] St. Augustine said: "Just as we specifically call the one Word of God with the name 'wisdom' so too, in a general way, also the Spirit is specifically called the name 'charity' (love), even though the Father and the Son, are in a general way, also charity.'"[18]

How Then Shall We Understand the Three?

William of St. Thierry said we do not become God but we become what God is in virtue of his own nature. Since God's nature is love, and love comes from God, we are transformed by this divine love. Through the grace of God we *become* what God is: love. This radical insight goes to the very root of our life in Christ. This is why Balthasar, in constructing his trinitarian theology of love, said: "God is not, in the first place, 'absolute power,' but 'absolute love' and his sovereignty manifests itself not in holding on to what is its own but in its abandonment—all this in such a way that the sovereignty displays itself in transcending the opposition, known to us from the world, between power and impotence."[19]

> There is no fear in love, but perfect love casts out fear; for fear has to do with punishment, and whoever fears has not reached perfection in love. We love because he first loved us. Those who say, "I love God," and hate a brother or sister are liars, for those who do not love a brother or sister, whom they have seen, cannot love God, whom they have not seen. (1 John 4:18–20)

Thus we cannot "hate" our brother and truly love God. I submit that we cannot truly love God until we know how much God truly loves us.

---

16. Cerini, *God Who is Love*, 26.
17. Pope John Paul II, cited by Cerini, *God Who is Love*, 81.
18. Augustine, *Trinitate,* cited by Cerini, *God Who is Love*, 81.
19. Clements, *Meaning of the World is Love*, 45–46.

His love for us is shown most fully in the Trinity, where we receive love through the gift of the Father, the life of the Son, and the continual work and power of the Holy Spirit.

Why the Trinity Matters for Divine Love

One of the most consequential New Testament texts on the mystery of God sums up what we have seen in this chapter, reminding us that what we are dealing with here is an attempt to explain the greatness of God's being and love in the Trinity (1 Tim 3:14–16).

> I hope to come to you soon, but I am writing these instructions to you so that, if I am delayed, you may know how one ought to behave in the household of God, which is the church of the living God, the pillar and support of the truth. Without any doubt, the mystery of godliness is great:
> He was revealed in flesh,
> vindicated in spirit,
> seen by angels,
> proclaimed among gentiles,
> believed in throughout the world,
> taken up in glory.

The Scottish Reformed theologian T. F. Torrance said of this text:

> [This] was a passage that came to play a central and important role in formulating the doctrine of the Trinity. Understood in light of the overarching framework of God's self-revelation as Father, Son and Holy Spirit, this mystery of godliness or godly worship came to mean thinking of God in an essentially *trinitarian* way, so that the equation theology = godliness . . . was identified with trinitarian thinking or simply with the worship and doctrine of the Holy Trinity.[20]

As we saw above, God seeks a relationship with us that can rightly be called "deified union."[21] The fourteenth-century mystic Julian of Norwich wrote: "God wishes to be known, and is pleased that we should rest in him."[22] As we've seen there are real limitations on what a finite being can understand about divine love. But we've also seen that God's inner

---

20. Torrance, *Christian Doctrine of God, One Being Three Persons*, 74.
21. Wessling, *Love Divine*, 245.
22. Spearing, *Revelations of Divine Love*, 47.

The Trinity of Love

life is perfect eternal love. A deeply interpersonal knowledge of God's life can be *experienced* because of the doctrine of participation.

Paul said there was a veil over the face of Moses when he came down from the mountain with the law of God. Why? "The people of Israel could no more look at him than stare into the sun" (2 Cor 3:8, MSG). But when those brought to God by the Spirit under the new covenant experienced the glory there was "nothing to hide" (2 Cor 3:12, MSG) What follows is nothing short of amazing love (2 Cor 3:16–18).

What then is the veil that Paul speaks of? It is the spiritual and mental covering that hides God's glory. The "glory of the Lord" (Exod 33:18–19) is the biblical designation for God's character. Paul says this veil is removed in Christ. Simply put, the character of God is revealed in the life and death of Jesus Christ. Paul further explains this by adding: "God once said, 'Let the light shine out of the darkness!' This is the same God who made his light shine in our hearts by letting us know the glory of God that is in the face of Christ" (2 Cor 4:6, New Century Version). So it is Jesus who "reflects the glory of God and shows exactly what God is like" (Heb. 1:3, New Century Version). There is one clear way to behold the love of God—focus your mind and heart on God's love. As the light of God's love penetrates our minds and hearts we grow in our love for him. (Some steps we can take to move closer into this love will be explained in chapter 15.)

Kallistos Ware concludes that ultimately we can only *hint* at the paradox of the Trinity in human language. Why? It will always be beyond our words and human understanding. "Our reasoning powers are a gift from God, and we must use them to the full; but we should recognize their limitations."[23] The Trinity is most definitely *not* a philosophical theory. It is the *revelation* of the living God who is perfect love.

At the end of the day, the best analogy of the Trinity we have is not well known by modern Christians. *This analogy is rooted in the love of persons in a relationship.*[24]

Chiara Lubich was right when she concluded that God-Love is a trinitarian *giving of self* on the part of God-Love for us.[25] God created us out of love and redeems out of love. He gives us the Holy Spirit so we can participate in divine love eternally. This trinitarian love empowers us—through the Holy Spirit who is often designated as "love"—to receive

23. Ware, *Orthodox Way*, 31.
24. Ware, *Orthodox Way*, 29.
25. Cerini, *God Who Is Love*, 57.

the virtues of faith, hope, and love. The *way* we participate in these virtues through the incarnation and the Trinity remains a mystery but this glorious mystery is what gives us real hope. What is given is God-Love himself, the God who floods our soul with the fire and the light that transforms. We live love because we first know God-Love!

The Witness of Julian of Norwich: "All Shall Be Well"

One of the best-known reflections on divine love in the history of the church was written by the fourteenth-century English mystic Julian of Norwich (1343–1416). Thomas Merton said Julian was "without doubt one of the most wonderful of all Christian voices." The former Archbishop of Canterbury, Rowan Williams, said Julian's writings "may well be the most important work of Christian reflection in the English language."[26] I have come to agree with this assessment.

It would appear to us moderns, in the light of our contemporary understanding of what we call a "near death experience," that Julian came to death's door and underwent a great discovery. Her discovery led to written reflections on the love she experienced. When later faced with real doubt she replied in words that are widely known: "It was necessary that there should be sin; but all shall be well, and all shall be well, and all manner of thing shall be well." There is my thesis again!

Julian believed that all the love of God was mirrored in the death of Christ. But she just as firmly held to trinitarian teaching by seeing that each person of the Trinity—Father, Son, and Holy Spirit—fully indwells the others in love; they are distinct but never separate. Julian did not interpret the passion as the Father acting upon the Son, as some medieval theologians did, and as many evangelicals still do. She understood that one person of the holy Trinity cannot act against another. This would fracture the communion of divine love.[27]

Julian also understood that in eternity past God embraced and enfolded all human life into his divine being. This is the way divine love heals, restores and receives us without condition or merit. She believed God not only loves us but he actually likes us. We should put our trust in this "liking and love" of God because God takes great delight in us and will be gentle with us beyond description.

---

26. Earle, *Julian of Norwich,* from the back cover of the book.
27. Earle, *Julian of Norwich,* 76.

The Trinity of Love

I saw that God never began to love humankind, for just as humankind shall be in eternal bliss, completing the joy of God in his own works, so has that same humankind been in God's foresight, known and loved according to God's righteous purpose before time began. And by the eternal consent and agreement of the whole Trinity, Christ would be the ground and head of these fair beings, he from whom we all come, in whom we are all enclosed, into whom we shall return; finding in him our full heaven and everlasting joy through the foreseeing purpose of the whole blessed Trinity since before time began. Before he made us he loved us, and when we were made we loved him; and this is a love made of the essential goodness natural to the Holy Ghost [Spirit], mighty by reason of the might of the Father, and wise in accordance with the wisdom of the Son. Thus man's soul is made of God and bound to God by the same ties.[28]

---

28. Earle, *Julian of Norwich*, 79.

Chapter Thirteen

Amazing Love
The Death and Resurrection of Christ

> Love must be a quality in the character, the nature
> of God, which is thus revealed in God's loving deeds,
> and especially in the atoning work of Christ.
> —Geoffrey Grogan

> Let none fear death, for the death of the Savior has
> set us free. Christ has risen and the demons have
> fallen. Christ has risen and the angels rejoice.
> —St. John Chrysostom

> For as we lost the sure word of God by means of a tree, by
> means of a tree again was it made manifest to all, showing the
> height, the length, the breadth, the depth in itself . . . through
> the extension of the hands of a divine person.
> —Irenaeus

WE HAVE NOW SEEN how the goodness and kindness of God (Titus 3:4–5) leads us to conclude that the God who saves us is love. We have also seen that we were created because of God's love. Every breath we draw comes from this same God-Love. Yet we have tragically used our God-given freedom to sin. We have become estranged and painfully turned inward. We don't like to recognize it but this is the necessary beginning of the Spirit's work in renewing us. God's love in Christ seeks us and gives us new life, a life which leads us to surrender to this amazing love.

Jesus's Death and Resurrection

In chapter 11 we saw *how* God has been revealed in human flesh. We saw in the chapter 12 that God is love in Trinity. As such God's love is a dynamic relationship of three. These profound truths have a great bearing on the transforming power of love. Now we need to consider the importance of Christ's death and resurrection for our experience of divine love.

We begin by again noting that all serious Christian theology recognizes the utter *centrality* of Jesus Christ. Here is love revealed in human flesh; here is love crucified; and so here is love risen from the dead! Paul can say: "For I resolved to know nothing while I was with you except Jesus Christ and him crucified" (1 Cor 2:2). The words "Jesus Christ and him crucified" became Paul's shorthand way to describe his entire ministry. In the New Testament the great central truth is the death of Christ. (This death always leads to Christ's resurrection; these two truths *cannot* be separated.)

Here then is love—love dies and love rises! Here again is the truth of John 3:16. God so loved the world that he *gave* his only-begotten Son in order that the world might know his love. If we want to know the mind and heart of Jesus we must see him as the revealer of God's nature. Jesus, as Brad Jersak has accurately said, reveals a more "Christlike God."[1] If you understand this it will settle a number of other questions.

When I ponder the love of Christ crucified and risen I find myself singing the words of Charles Wesley's beloved hymn: "And Can It Be That I Should Gain?" His words express my confidence in love: "Amazing love! How can it be that thou my God should die for me?"

Indeed, Christ's death is amazing love!

---

1. Jersak, *More Christlike God.*

"God Took a Risk"

In chapter 4 we saw that God created us in his image and likeness. But humankind used the freedom God gave us to walk away from trusting and loving God. Sin is thus common to us all and sin is deeply personal. It has fragmented us from both ourselves and our neighbors. We are sick and need a great physician.

At this point I return to the question I posed at the beginning of this book: "Why did God create us with the possibility of sin in the first place?" After all, sin brings death and suffering. So why would a God of love permit it? We find no *completely* satisfactory answer in the Bible. Still we ask, "Why?" I answer—because God is the God of love! "Love implies sharing, and love also implies freedom. As the Trinity of love, God desired to share his life with created persons made in his image. Such persons were made to be capable of responding to him freely and willingly in a relationship of love."[2] We could not truly love him if we were coerced to do so. Why? Because where there is no freedom there cannot be true love. "God can do everything except compel us to love him. God, therefore—desiring to share his love—created, not robots who would obey him mechanically, but angels and human beings endowed with free choice. . . . God took a risk."[3]

I love Kallistos Ware's expression here: *God took a risk!*

Humankind's original sin was turning from God-centeredness to self-centeredness. The *desire* to be like God was not the real problem. In fact, I submit this desire was good. The problem was that our first parents sought to fulfill this desire through self-centeredness. We do the same. The result of our self-centeredness is what the Bible means by the word "sin." Sin causes us to see ourselves and others in terms of our own satisfaction and personal pleasure. The physical effects of this way of life are pain, disease, and death. "Yet (even) physical death should be seen, not primarily as a punishment, but as a means of release provided by a loving God. In his mercy God did not want us to go on living indefinitely in a fallen world . . . for death is not the end of life but the beginning of its renewal."[4]

As we saw earlier the way the church understood the effects of the fall have not been uniform. In the West we speak of "depravity," even of "total depravity" in some circles. In the East it is believed that the divine

---

2. Ware, *Orthodox Way*, 58.
3. Ware, *Orthodox Way*, 58–59, quote from Paul Evdokimov.
4. Ware, *Orthodox Way*, 60.

image was obscured but never obliterated.[5] What we must understand is that the one source of life is always God himself. Every living thing has life in God. Physical death is not our end. We look beyond death, not to a heaven in the skies, but rather to the reunion of the body and soul at the general resurrection on the last day.

> The doctrine of original sin means rather that we are born into an environment where it is easy to do evil and hard to do good; easy to hurt others, and hard to heal their wounds; easy to arouse men's suspicions, and hard to win their trust. It means that we are each of us conditioned by the solidarity of the human race in its accumulated wrong-doing and wrong thinking, and hence wrong-being. And to this accumulation of wrong *we have ourselves added by our own deliberate acts of sin*. The gulf grows wider and wider" (italics mine).[6]

Reconciling the World

Paul has rightly been called the greatest apostle of the gospel. Having met Christ in a blinding vision on the road to Damascus (Acts 9:27), Saul (who would soon become Paul, the apostle to the gentiles) was totally transformed by the gospel after he saw and heard Jesus speak healing to him. (Notice again: love is revealed in light!) Paul writes: "For the message about the cross is foolishness to those who are perishing, but to us who are being saved it is *the power of God* (1 Cor 1:18). He knew the power of Christ when he wrote: "In Christ God was reconciling the world to himself" (2 Cor. 5:19). Paul's gospel can be summarized in a *shorthand* way. "May I never boast of anything except *the cross* of our Lord Jesus Christ, by which the world has been crucified to me and I to the world" (Gal 6:14). *The cross, on which Jesus died, is the gospel!* The cross reconciles the world to God! Paul concludes that "Jesus gave himself for our sins *to set us free* from the present evil age, according to the will of our God and Father" (Gal 1:4). We must conclude that God sent Christ to deal with sin once for all. The writer to the Hebrews sums this up saying: "For then he would have had to suffer again and again since the foundation of the world. But as it is, he has appeared *once for all* at the end of the ages to *remove sin by the sacrifice of himself*" (Heb 9:26). It is surely right to conclude that the

---

5. Ware, *Orthodox Way*, 61.
6. Ware, *Orthodox Way*, 62.

Father suffers no less than the Son because he did not *withhold* his own Son but rather *gave him up* for us all and *suffered with him.*

A straightforward reading of the New Testament makes it abundantly clear that the writers used *diverse imagery* to convey the meaning of Christ's death. It is wholly incorrect to suggest that the cross "awakens" God's love. We should rather say: "The cross is the fruit of God's love."[7]

Indeed, the cross is the event that fully reveals the fullness of the truth that "God is love."

There is no sense in which God sent Jesus to do a task that he was not prepared to undertake himself. The all too common idea that an angry God demanded justice therefore he had to kill his own Son on our behalf is so foreign to the love of God that it still surprises me how many Christians think this is what the death of Christ actually means. (In my case I heard this idea for so long that it was hard to think otherwise.) This idea looks more like "divine child abuse" than the love of God. My former professor, the esteemed New Testament scholar Leon Morris, rightly said, "Sometimes, in their anxiety to give due emphasis to what Christ has done for us, Evangelicals have unwittingly introduced a division in the Godhead."[8]

A Modern Controversy

When the Presbyterian Church (USA) wanted to edit a line in a very popular contemporary song ("In Christ Alone"), so as to include it in their new church hymnal, a big debate ensued. The original line said: "Till on that cross as Jesus died, the wrath of God was satisfied." What was put in place of this line read: "As Jesus died, the love of God was magnified." Here is the entire second verse of this very popular song:

> In Christ alone, Who took on flesh,
> Fullness of God in helpless babe!
> This gift of love and righteousness,
> Scorned by the ones He came to save.
> Till on that cross as Jesus died,
> The wrath of God was satisfied;
> For ev'ry sin on Him was laid—
> Here in the death of Christ I live.[9]

---

7. Thiselton, *Thiselton Companion to Christian Theology*, 63.
8. Morris, *Glory in the Cross*, 46–47.
9. "In Christ Alone," words and music by Keith Getty and Stuart Townsend.

This change was not significantly challenged until a well-respected Baptist theologian raised an objection in the magazine *First Things*.[10] His objection was quite strong. He saw this change as a capitulation to liberalism. This debate is rooted in the atonement theology of wrath, which says God must substitute Christ in our place so as to be *satisfied* by the death of Christ and turn aside from his wrath against us. But is this right?

Interestingly this story was covered by many Christian magazines, both Catholic and Protestant. It even made the *Washington Post, USA Today,* and *The Economist*. Rarely does such a theological controversy attract this much attention. So why? Undoubtedly the disagreement over the meaning of the atonement, as seen in the line "the wrath of God was satisfied," touched a very deep nerve. Conservatives, especially Calvinistic ones, felt strongly that the work of Christ on the cross was being undermined by this word change. Many embarked upon a response that suggested this change introduced heresy. (To be truthful I agree with both sides when they say that most Christians do not even see, much less understand, what this disagreement is all about.) However, I do not think this line is essential to the nature of God or to a healthy doctrine of the cross. But why?

How Then Shall We Understand the Atonement?

It is incumbent upon me to say that faithful theologians have always offered different explanations for *why* it was necessary for Christ to die. When any one theory has been used to explain *the answer* to this question of why Christ died we easily go astray. These various ideas are called "theories of the atonement" for good reason. They are just that—theories. The early church, for example, did not believe in this idea of atonement that we in the West regularly fight about when we debate words in songs like "In Christ Alone." Most Orthodox teaching treated Christ's death as the *satisfaction* "of God's truth."

James R. Payton Jr., an evangelical Reformed Christian, ably states the Orthodox position.

> The divine warning to our first parents that disobedience would result in death had come to pass; sin and death had passed on to all humanity; and the cycle of sin and death had continued.

---

10. Timothy George, "No Squishy Love," Parts 1 and 2, in *First Things*, July 29 and August 26, 2013.

(See Gen, 2:17; Rom. 5:12; 6:23). Since Christ had never sinned, he did not have to die himself. However, those "in him" are and would be sinners for whom death must come as the consequence of sin. As the last Adam, the new head of a renewed humanity, Christ took on himself the death that should befall all those in him. In so doing, he satisfied God's truth. Because of the death of Christ, that truth is not violated when those who are sinners receive everlasting life. In this manner, the Eastern Christian tradition speaks of Christ's death as satisfaction.[11]

Add to this excellent historic approach to the cross, and the doctrine of satisfaction, the simple fact that the early Greek church fathers believed that a ransom was paid to the devil. (This shocks modern evangelicals but few even know the teaching of the early church on the death of Christ.) Christ's death was understood as Christ offering himself to Satan in the place of humankind. Satan had dominion over humanity and Christ "set us free." Satan achieved this power over human beings through the deception of our first parents. But God stripped the devil of his dominion and robbed the strongman's house (cf. Mark 3:27). A careful reading of the Gospels shows how this idea works itself out in the human story.

We may not be able to fully explain *why* Christ died, or precisely what transpired through his death, but we can and must conclude that Jesus died in order to save us from our sin. *His death really saves us.* This is not in dispute! I personally wish Christians would stop attacking other Christians about every aspect of our interpretation of this central truth.

The entire chapter of Isaiah 53, written centuries before the death of Jesus, quite clearly says the Messiah died to save us. Here is only one verse from this well-known chapter: "But he was wounded for our transgressions, crushed for our iniquities; upon him was the punishment that made us whole, and by his bruises we are healed" (Isa 53:5). This sounds a lot like the Father punished the Son in order to save us. But in my estimation the Catholic philosopher Peter Kreeft sees this message of the cross more clearly.

> The Cross gives us not only salvation but also knowledge of salvation, not only God's love but the knowledge of God's love. If He has not done this unthinkable deed of love—a thing no saint, no prophet, no apostle understood or expected—how would we have known what perfect love is? What other event in history, what other concept that has ever been conceived, has ever told

---

11. Payton Jr., *Light from the Christian East*, 126.

us what love is as radically as the Cross? The Cross is how Christ made the Father known most completely.[12]

The Doctrine of Substitution

As I have noted many times I was raised in a Protestant context. I was taught the doctrine called penal substitutionary atonement. This teaching lies at the heart of most modern debates about the meaning of Christ's death. This idea was first developed by St. Anselm, who taught a satisfaction theory of the atonement.[13] His idea was that the death of Christ was the only rationally intelligible way in which sinful humankind could be reconciled with God. This teaching directly impacted the development of a particular kind of Catholic theology. In this view the death of Christ was *necessary* to remove the wrath of God. Many of the heirs of the Protestant Reformers also taught this doctrine of *penal substitutionary atonement*. This idea can be seen in words such as these: "For Christ also died for sins once for all, the righteous for the unrighteous, that he might bring us to God" (1 Pet 3:18).But is this idea of *penal* substitution correct when it says the Father had to violently punish and kill Jesus (or at least *direct* the events of his crucifixion) in order to satisfy and appease his own divine wrath? This thinking led to a type of preaching I embraced for several decades. In my context I believed that this was the *only* way to preach the gospel since this was the right way to see *how* Christ saves us.

Over time I realized that this language of violence pictured God as both abusive and violent. I began to question if this idea was radically inconsistent with the nature of God as love. Parts of the basis for this view can clearly be found within the Bible but I submit that the *total witness* of Scripture, with its various metaphors and images, is based upon something like this well-known text in Leviticus: "For the life of the flesh is in the blood, and I have given it to you for making atonement for your lives on the altar, for, as life, it is the blood that makes atonement" (17:11). Since blood is "the life of the flesh" this atonement language requires blood. But the apparent point is that Jesus sacrificed his life for us! Blood is generally associated with life and death, even in modern culture.

---

12. Kreeft, *God Who Loves You*, 130.

13. A fine article on the various theories of atonement, and their development, can be found online at: https://en.wikipedia.org/wiki/Category:Atonement_in_Christianity

I now see a way to better understand the various biblical metaphors for the death of Christ. The late Protestant theologian Colin Gunton (1943–2003) helped me better understand how these biblical metaphors regarding the death of Christ should lead to insights that prosaic literalism can never attain. "As we move from one family of metaphors to another, we must be aware that they do not operate in self-controlled worlds."[14] In this same vein the great German Lutheran theologian Joachim Jeremias saw at least six diverse fields of thought—thus images—for the atonement. His six were: (1) sacrificial language, (2) metaphors for redemption, (3) forensic themes, (4) an ethical image seen in Christ's vicarious obedience, (5) the language of transference, and (6) reconciliation.

Peter Kreeft provides a simple example of how to sum up what we've seen.

> Suppose you had an ant farm, and the ants rebelled against you. Suppose that somehow or other, the only way you could save the ants from the terrible results of their own folly was to become an ant and be killed by the rebel ants. How much love would you have to have to do this? Not nearly as much as God had. The distance He came, from the infinite to the finite, is infinitely farther than the distance you would have to go to become an ant. This remote and somewhat ridiculous analogy barely gives us a glimpse of the total shock and the utter surprise felt by the first disciples when they realized what God had done for them.
>
> We could never have known how unthinkably large and wide and deep God's love is but for the cross.[15]

Paul express this glorious truth clearly in 2 Corinthians 5:17–19.

> So if anyone is in Christ, there is a new creation: everything old has passed away; look, new things have come into being! All this is from God, who reconciled us to himself through Christ and has given us the ministry of reconciliation; that is, in Christ God was reconciling the world to himself, not counting their trespasses against them, and entrusting the message of reconciliation to us.

God did not dangle sinners over the pit of hell just waiting to punish them. And he surely did not *punish* his Son *in order* to forgive us. Paul says God "reconciled us to himself through Christ." He first loved us and then gave up his only Son to save us by showing us just how much he

---

14. Gunton, *Actuality of the Atonement*, 27–52, 83.
15. Kreeft, *God Who Loves You*, 130–31.

really loved us. But using this vivid imagery of the cross in a crassly literal way can be grossly misleading. I also believe it confounds the real truth of Jesus' death—a death suffered because of eternal love.

For the Love of God

"Each event in the life of Christ—each incident in the Gospels—is a note on the main theme of the biblical love song. It would be possible to show this love at work in every detail and every event in the pages of the four Gospels."[16] You cannot really know how much God loves you until you "see" this to be true. Yes, Jesus is an example for us to follow but this is *not* the principle reason for his incarnation, death, and resurrection. The Son of God became man in order to die! One of the most baffling texts in all the New Testament underscores this point in a stark way (Luke 12:49–53). Here Christ spoke openly of the baptism he must undergo (Luke 12:50). Yet we know he had already been baptized in water by John the Baptist several years before he spoke these words. So what is he referring to? (It appears he is even impatient for this baptism to happen.) I now believe it is abundantly clear that he is referring here to his death as *the baptism of the cross!*

But why does this baptism figure so prominently? (Please understand that Jesus is not welcoming death in a psychologically warped sense.) He longs for the cross for two reasons. First, it was for love and obedience to his Father who had sent him to fulfill this mission. In allowing the Roman Empire to assert control over his life God revealed that his power is in the cross; i.e., the power of divine weakness (2 Cor 12:9). Second, it was for his love for you and me. "Christ loved us and gave himself up for us" (Eph 5:2).

Love Suffers and Dies

In the account of the transfiguration we saw Jesus' clear announcement of his coming resurrection: "As they were coming down the mountain, he ordered them to tell no one about what they had seen, until after the Son of Man had *risen* from the dead" (Mark 9:9). (The three disciples were not yet able to understand such a stupendous truth.) In Luke's Gospel we see that when the resurrection was announced the effect it had on

16. Kreeft, *God Who Loves You*, 129.

the women who first heard this angelic message was astounding: "The women were terrified and bowed their faces to the ground, but the men [angels] said to them, 'Why do you look for the living among the dead? He is not here but has risen'" (Luke 24:5).

Consider the story itself and the central truths contained in it. "Because Christ our God is true man, he died a full and genuine human death upon the cross. But because he was not only true man but true God, because he is life itself and the source of life, this death was not and could not be the final conclusion."[17]

It often puzzles those who first hear the Christian story that we believe Jesus' death was a victory. What is called Good Friday was really "good." But why? Because here we see the love of God in Christ's dying. The Creed says this with an economy of words: "Suffered under Pontius Pilate."

All of this creates a distinct picture in our minds. But the picture many of us have embraced can be quite monstrous. "The redemption was carried out *in* suffering. But must we believe that it was by *means* of that suffering? This is really the crux of the problem."[18]

So I ask: "Does suffering have value in itself?" The answers many Christians give make it sound like it does. But Jesus never taught this for he said, "Love one another" not "mortify one another." Yes, our redemption was achieved through sacrifice, thus we should ask: "What is this sacrifice?"

Sacrifice does not mean to do something bad in order to please God. It means to do something "sacred" (*sacrum facere*), to make something God's by consecration. Yet we routinely translate sacrifice to mean loss, deprivation, destruction. To sacrifice something is to give it utmost value, even to divinize it. To sacrifice means to love more, to reverence more. When we love our spouse, for example, we sacrifice. We consecrate ourselves for love. This is the basic idea I now believe we need to recover.

Sin is *repaired* through Christ's sacrifice. But this sacrifice is wholly the work of God-Love, a work of love on the part of the Father, who far from demanding a ransom of suffering from us, loves us so much that he sends his Son to bring us back to himself. "A work of love on the part of the Son, who reveals himself to us, not because he suffers, but because he loves. He reveals to us the love we have lost, and he communicates that love to all who open themselves to it."[19]

17. Ware, *Orthodox Way*, 83.
18. Evely, *Credo*, 92.
19. Evely, *Credo*, 93.

It is precisely because redemption is a work in amazing love that it takes place through Christ's sufferings. *Real love always involves suffering.* "The magnificence of Christ's passion truly lies in the fact that it was not an act of asceticism, a planned mortification, a wished-for mutilation, but simply love being faithful." If you wish to unite yourself to his death in the Spirit then unite yourself to this love. Do not try to suffer more. Suffering is not meritorious. It does not earn divine favor. *It consecrates true love!* True love lasts, true love remembers. True love offers oneself in order to give life.[20]

So how should we meditate on the suffering of Christ? The answer to this question has led the church to embrace a variety of responses, some more helpful than others in my understanding. We must reject this idea: that by imagining Christ as being stricken by the Father's anger we will grow in grace. Imagine Christ as sustained in his suffering by the love of the Father and realize with utter reverence and joy that it was inexhaustible love that led him to die in our place. Ponder this mystery deeply.

> Christ on the cross was doing the same as in heaven: loving. When he was crucified, Christ was simply accomplishing here, in his distant provinces, amid the tumult of the elements, what he does unceasingly in his own dwelling-place in glory and joy. He gave thanks, he gave himself into his Father's hands. For an instant, in the course of the ages, heaven was opened, and we could contemplate the eternal happiness of God, the intensity of joy, the power of his love. Our names for this are crucifixion, passion, cross, sacrifice; what it really was was love and happiness.[21]

It is plain to me that the first Christians, as well as those who came after them, centered their message in God's love, a love seen preeminently in the death and resurrection of Jesus of Nazareth. In fact, it was this core belief that led to their persecution. The first Christians actually believed that the whole of their testimony was to become witnesses of Christ's resurrection (Acts 2:32). They did not mess around with Greek ideas about the soul without the body but pointedly said to their critics: "You killed the author of life, whom God raised from the dead. To this we are witnesses" (Acts 3:15). And when they were arrested and brought before the Sanhedrin they replied that this was for the truth of the resurrection

---

20. Evely, *Credo*, 93.
21. Evely, *Credo*, 99–100.

(Acts 5:27–32). Paul said the very essence of Christian faith is to believe that Jesus Christ was raised from the dead (1 Cor 15:12–19).

Christ's resurrection is central to Christian faith for a number of reasons but the most important can be easily missed. *His resurrection is ours.* The eternal hope that we have is not in this life, nor is it in going to heaven when we die. Our true hope is in the risen Christ who as the head of all mankind will raise us on the last day (1 Cor 15:22). He is called the Last Adam for a reason (1 Cor 15:45).

In my background the historical fact of Jesus' resurrection became an Easter apologetic. The central defense of the faith was to show that Jesus was risen. But the central truth of the resurrection is that Christ risen touches every person who comes into the world. It is of *first importance* because it is *the beginning* of the eternal truth of resurrection for all persons in him.

Love Rises from the Dead for Us

Paul is abundantly clear: Christians believe Christ is risen! John said Christ came in human flesh (1 John 4:2). We can now see that these two truths are really two parts of the same truth. The resurrection and the incarnation are essentially the same mystery. "The resurrection is the incarnation perpetuated, but in flesh that is incorruptible and life-giving."[22]

We must further see that the resurrection means Christ's death was not a suicide.

> There is nothing morbid or selfish about it. In going to the Cross, the Son of God chose life, not death. The movement of his will was in perfect accord with the will of the Father of Life, consistent with his unlimited love for humankind. With his arms outstretched, Christ beckons humankind to join him on his cross, which is at the center of the universe and on which life triumphs over death in his person.[23]

Thus we can see that God's love *is* God's power in resurrection. There is no *meaningful* distinction here—as I hinted at earlier when I spoke of the power of God—between God's weakness and God's power (1 Cor 1:15). For that matter, there is no difference between God's will and God's love (1 John 3:16). Vigen Guroian is surely right: "God's love

---

22. Evely, *Credo*, 101.
23. Guroian, *Melody of Faith*, 96.

is the height of God's power. In other words: God's love is power and his power is love." The sixth-century Orthodox philosopher David Anhaght adds, "The One who alone is real has in Him as His own each and all the powers."[24] For this reason the death of Jesus on the cross did not lead to the demise of Christ but rather to the resurrection, which is the victory and the power of the cross. The crucifixion led to the resurrection. I lived most of my life not seeing this absolutely essential truth about *how* Christ's death and resurrection were *united* in God's love and purpose.

> Thus, the Crucifixion could not possibly have led to the demise of Jesus Christ, but only to his resurrection. For indeed, the power of the Resurrection is the power of the Cross. Henceforth, every cross is a crucifix, and every crucifix is the victorious Cross. *The Crucifixion did not make the Resurrection necessary; rather, in order that the Resurrection might come to pass, the Crucifixion had to be.* The aim and goal of Christ's sufferings and death is resurrection. "For though He was crucified in weakness, yet He lives by the power of God (2 Cor. 13:4, NKJV).[25]

But how many Christians understand that the resurrection is not about the Greek idea of the immortality of the soul? I constantly hear Christians speak about going to heaven with little emphasis on the resurrection. Paul teaches us how to rightly understand the resurrection in 1 Corinthians 15. *It is the whole person, both body and spirit, that will receive immortality in our future resurrection.*

Most religions treat death as the mortal soul's great liberator from the prison of the body. But, "In the Christian faith . . . death is the great despoiler of the creature whom God has made in his very own image, whom he has made for eternal life." This means that "The human person is not just a soul, for then he is a ghost; nor is he simply a physical body, for then he is a corpse. The human person is a body-and-soul unity, and death sunders this unity. This is the meaning of corruption of which St. Paul speaks."[26]

So what does love have to do with these central truths of the Christian faith? At his resurrection Christ did not simply roll away the stone from his tomb; he abolished all the barriers enclosing us in our prisons— the prisons of class, of race, of language, of time, of place, of distance, and

---

24. Guroian, *Melody of Faith*, 97.
25. Guroian, *Melody of Faith*, 97–98.
26. Gurorian, *Melody of Faith*, 129.

of sex. The glory of the risen Christ is that he has broken down the walls of division and hatred. So Paul says: "There is no longer Jew or Greek; there is no longer slave or free; there is no longer male and female, for all of you are one in Christ Jesus" (Gal 3:28).

In entering human history God has shattered all previous conceptions of who and what God is like! In the revealing light of God's perfect and eternal love for us we can now clearly see the true greatness of Jesus. Indeed, what we see in the death and resurrection of Jesus is amazing love! Charles Wesley rightly asked, "How can it be that Thou my God should die for me?"

When the New Testament speaks of the resurrection of Christ it always does so in the center of human reality itself. This means the resurrection is not simply talking about the reality of being raised as an event, as an objective fact (which I believe it is). The resurrection speaks to me passionately about participating in his resurrection and learning to live out from it. "The Gospels aim to bring their readers into a relationship with the crucified and risen Lord."[27]

Alexander Schmemann (1921–1983) has done perhaps as much as any twentieth-century theologian to open minds and hearts in the West to Orthodox insights about the death and resurrection of divine love in Jesus Christ. Schmemann wrote: "He who is life itself, descends to death out of love and co-suffering, descends to a death which he did not create, which has taken over the world and poisoned life."[28]

---

27. Kelly, *God Is Love*, 51.
28. Schmemann, *Celebration of Faith*, 86.

Chapter Fourteen

Misconceptions

> Let us remember this: God judges us by loving us.
> —Pope Francis

> Abiding conceptions of God recur throughout history and theology. Some of them may even compete with the Bible itself.
> —Bradley Jersak

> When you light somebody afire with the grace of God, you have a hard time putting him out. When you light people with legalism or with rules and regulations, they're going to burn out because they'll always live in fear. But a person set on fire with the love of Jesus Christ will live in gratitude—serving his Lord out of love not out of fear.
> —Max Lucado

IT SHOULD BE ABUNDANTLY clear by now that most of us embraced images of God, whether knowingly or unknowingly. I mean, "How do you explain God to a child?" These images range widely over the ground of diverse perspectives regarding God's love. I was reminded of this recently when a conversation with my seven-year-old twin grandsons led to a talk about our "seeing" God. Explaining to my boys that God is there but we cannot "see" him with our physical eyes presented the usual challenges. The fact is, we all form mental images through the way we think about God whether we are seven or seventy-five. These images influence how we talk, how we think, and especially how we worship and pray. Some of the more common ideas we have of God include four very common ones cited by Bradley Jersak in his magnificent book *A More Christlike God*.

1. The doting grandpa
2. The deadbeat dad
3. The punitive judge
4. The curious Santa Claus blend.[1]

Jersak says these four misconceptions have competed with one another throughout Christian history. All four have some support within the Bible itself. But these images are all un-Christlike. "Unhealthy ideas about God are often rooted in the bitterness of our own hearts. People instinctively push their highest expectations and deepest disappointments onto God, especially when their hearts are somehow afflicted or infected with sorrows."[2] Consider each of these common examples of an un-Christlike image of God.

1. The Doting Grandfather

This view begins with the idea that love means God is "nice." He even seems rather naive. We can imagine God spoiling his grandchildren by giving them whatever they want. He turns a blind eye to their misbehavior. We confess our sins and instantly God gives us the blessings we desire.

Let me illustrate how this idea affected me growing up in a Christian home. One of the verses I learned as a young child was: "Take delight in the Lord, and he will give you the desires of your heart" (Ps 37:4). My mom taught me this verse when I began asking about my sense of God calling me to be a minister. The words of Jesus teach us that "Whatever you ask

---

1. Jersak, *More Christlike God*, 25. See chapter 2, where I draw my ideas for this chapter.
2. Jersak, *More Christlike God*, 32.

for in prayer with faith, you will receive" (Matt 21:22). This obviously underscores the idea of "receiving" gifts and blessings we deeply desire. Surely, we can say there are wonderful promises in God's Word. But have we rightly understood these verses? "[These promises] are also perilous. There are two deep ditches to avoid here. On one side, we might infer a 'whatever-you-want' fairytale God from these texts. And on the other, we might so over-react to them that we discard them as meaningless."[3]

There are so many ways that we can fall into these two ditches that I cannot enumerate them all here. I will give but one example of how this thinking plagued me in the past. In my forty-ninth year I began to feel weak and exhausted. I sought professional medical help. After several years I realized that I had a somewhat mysterious condition now recognized as chronic fatigue syndrome (CFS). I was very active traveling across American and overseas, preaching and teaching. But I was so exhausted that it was hard to press on. I reached the place where physicians could only treat my symptoms. They offered no cure. One doctor urged me to follow James 5:13–18, where the writer suggests a specific way to ask for healing. My hopes were very high for God to heal me. Pastors from the suburban Chicago area came to a meeting to pray over me. I was filled with hope. After all, James says Elijah prayed that it would not rain and it did not. Surely my CFS could be healed by Elijah's God. But as much as I desired healing it never happened. I had brief periods of relief. But over time these symptoms always returned. I wondered if I had confessed my sin properly. I asked God to show me if a dark secret of mine was behind this health condition. My mental anguish was often far worse than the physical suffering. Now, all these years later, CFS still plagues me. It leaves me with a profound struggle to live well.

As a young Christian I sometimes heard people say, "God said it, I believe it, that settles it." This is a great formula *if it works*! But formulas are generally *not* how God works in real life. I have learned a great deal through my suffering. I dare say many of my readers have as well. When life unravels where do you go for help? *What happens when God doesn't come through?* Jersak is helpful: "It strikes me that the same phenomenon occurs when we liberally use the phrase, 'the Lord told me,' to justify our own desires, only to have our hopes dashed on the cruelties of life."[4] Jersak expresses what happened when I embraced my affliction. "I was

---

3. Jersak, *More Christlike God*, 33.
4. Jersak, *More Christlike God*, 34.

tempted to swerve wildly into the other ditch." Believing in the absolute sovereignty of God I embraced a different idea, without articulating it at first. I reasoned that prayer doesn't really change things, it only changes me. The sovereign God wants me to submit and not ask for blessings. I tried other forms of prayer, such as the Serenity Prayer, contemplative prayers, praise and thank-you prayers. These were all helpful but none was entirely satisfactory. Why? *The Scriptures clearly exhort me to pray earnest, believing, and expectant prayers.* In a story Jersak tells about asking the late Eugene Peterson to help him with this conundrum, he says that Peterson told him when you don't see God directly answer there are two words that tell you what to do next: "Be disappointed." Risk disappointment! "Pray for heaven to touch earth and grieve because heaven is not earth."[5] I can summarize now how I eventually responded to my disappointments by quoting Jersak's own response:

> For me, staying between the ditches means learning how to empty myself of willfulness and to surrender my life (if only for a moment) to the supernatural love of God. . . . On my more courageous days, I tell him exactly what I'd like to see happen, but I leave the outcome to his love and care. He has enabled me to risk trusting again, whether the results are glorious or disappointing, because in either case, God is a loving Father who is always close.[6]

2. The Deadbeat Dad or Absentee Landlord

The second common false conception of God looks like a "deadbeat dad" or an "absentee landlord." This conception has never been a serious temptation for me. My father was busy but he always had time to show love for me. He did not express great affection easily but he showed just how much he cared by his consistently profound love. However, I have known many people over my years of pastoral care and counseling who experienced a terrible relationship with their father because he was absent or even hurtful. Some had a criminally abusive father. For these friends the pain of being forsaken continually impacts their spiritual lives. I think this is why deeply wounded souls often need considerable care. Healing

---

5. Jersak, *More Christlike God*, 37.
6. Jersak, *More Christlike God*, 37–38.

their inability to trust God as a good Father will likely require specific counseling and much prayer.

3. The Punitive Judge

The famous deist Voltaire, who actually gave us a number of useful insights, made an observation about God and Christians that is often all too accurate. "If God has created us in his image, we have more than reciprocated." My experience has revealed the truth of this saying. Too many angry and fearful religious people have imagined God to be just like them. It seems we cannot conceive of God being so much better than ourselves. Face it, if God loves us as much as I've argued it is really hard to believe this is true.

In the previous chapter we saw how various images of God as a judge impact us. Being "good enough" was never a serious temptation for me on one level. Yet on another I never felt like I had done enough for God. I was a perfectionist. This perfectionism remains a significant limp in my life to this day. My sense of God's judgment of sin only exacerbated this problem. What I did not understand for years was how this deeply flawed fear of God led me to more subtle forms of self-righteousness and judgmentalism. Without seeing it I embraced the idea that good behavior would be rewarded and bad behavior would be punished. I understood that my sin was atoned for "once for all" (Heb 9:12, 26) but I saw God's discipline of me as punitive.

Near my fortieth birthday I learned that my parents had been privately concerned that I might discover I was gifted and, as a result, become arrogant. Their fear was rooted in a form of piety that was not healthy. The problem was that I had felt the need to please God through my performance. Of course my performance was never enough. In my early adult life I embraced a form of Puritanism that led me to consistently "examine" my conscience in unhealthy ways. (I used 1 Peter 1:10 to go through my failures on a daily basis, seeking to make sure I truly belonged to Christ.) The sins I confessed were sometimes real but often I felt condemned by "general" guilt feelings. I have one memory, often powerfully brought up in my mind for some years, of taking advantage of a church policy by using a small book budget to buy several items that I *personally* wanted. When I left this church as a very young pastor (1972) I left these few books and Bibles on the shelf in my office.

But the sin of misusing the budget's purpose haunted me for decades. It would come up in my mind at the oddest times, always condemning me. I found peace only through continually embracing God's love and mercy. Remembrance of this sin no longer arises within me. I now wonder if this was sin and tend to think this got in the way of seeing and turning from my real sins, e.g., my lack of love for a few of my unpleasant members and my impatience with certain congregational habits of this small church.

Here are a few probing questions that might prove helpful for you to ask about God's judgment.

- Are you tormented by old guilt feelings about wrongs done? Are you stuck in remorse and regret no matter how sincerely you have tried to say "sorry"?
- Do internal voices accuse and condemn you for being "bad"? Do you punish yourself with hurtful words, such as "stupid," or exercise self-imposed consequences when you stumble?
- Do you ever inflict self-harm?
- Are you obsessed with measuring up or feel like you're just "not good enough"? Do you ever feel there's something wrong with you, but can't put your finger on it?
- Do you struggle with shame?
- When you imagine "judgment day," what do you expect? Does it cause fear? Does God welcome you and show his love?
- When circumstances don't go your way, do you think God is punishing you? When things go well, do you assume God is rewarding you? What does grace mean to you in that case?[7]

I am convinced now that some of these questions were a part of my life because I grew up in a pious background.[8] Remember my earlier reference to constant "rededication"? The truth is that "revivalism" deeply affected me. I have been told for over fifty years that I was a major catalyst for a campus revival at Wheaton College in February 1970. The memory of those days sometimes thrills me. Yet there were times when this remembrance condemned me. How could I not see more evidence for revival through my own long years of pastoral and international

---

7. Jersak, *More Christlike God*, 42–43.

8. This is not meant to reject all the good of my background, for which I am daily thankful. It is meant to give you some sense of my own story.

labor? Why do I not enjoy incredible influence now? Was that time in 1970 only a brief "shower" that was not really about God working through my life? This often leads me to feel like I'm trapped on a hamster wheel of guilt and grace.

I believe the popular writer Max Lucado asks the right questions about this common misconception of God. "Does the Word of God say, 'There is limited condemnation for those who are in Christ Jesus?' No. Does it say, 'There is some condemnation . . . '? No, it says, 'There is no condemnation for those who are in Christ Jesus.' Think of it—regardless of our sin, we are not guilty."[9] Amen!

If you read the Gospels carefully you will soon realize that Jesus' response to sinners was never condemnation. He invited sinners to come to him for rest. God has already judged your sin. In fact, you will not repent until you really believe that he already loves you and nothing you can do will change or add to that fact. God's judgment, which is real, is not punitive or retributive but corrective. Our supremely good Father has no desire to harm us. God's judgment happened through the cross. Pope Francis displayed a far more gracious message about this problem than I experienced in my anti-Catholic background. Read the words he spoke at his first Good Friday Mass.

> One word should suffice this evening that is the Cross itself. The Cross is the word through which God has responded to evil in the world . . . a word which is *love, mercy, forgiveness*. It also reveals a judgment. Namely, that God, in judging us, loves us. *Let us remember this God judges us by loving us.* If I embrace his love then I am saved. If I refuse it, then I am condemned, not by him, but by my own self, because God never condemns, he only loves and saves.[10]

4. The Santa Claus Blend

The fourth false image of God that Jersak gives is a blend of the other three. "Christmas has a powerful impact on children, who may laminate 'their theology of Santa' onto their idea of God when the two are held closely together on Christmas Eve."[11]

9. Lucado, *Walking*, no page number.

10. Pope Francis, "Way of the Cross." These words sum up my own conclusion very well.

11. Jersak, *More Christlike God*, 45.

Think about this idea of a Santa Claus blend. Santa is legalistic and judgmental. "He's keeping a list" and "checking it twice." And he's going to find out who's been naughty and nice. "He knows if you've been bad or good; So be good for goodness sake!" This thinking is entirely opposed to grace. But the flip side of this is that of the doting grandfather. We can get anything we ask for at Christmas just by asking. Have you ever taken your small children, in my case (more recently) my grandchildren, to see Santa in a department store? Santa asks the child what they want for Christmas and they believe he will deliver. Santa never disappoints. To put it mildly, this hodgepodge is a hybrid that employs some very false ideas about God. If God is love then this whole charade is wrong and should be abandoned.[12]

Two Primary Images of God

I have come to believe that we have inherited *two competing images of God* in Western culture. One is the God of pure will or freedom. This God has become a prosecuting attorney. The other image is of a God of pure love or goodness. "These two images clash within the 'biblical religions' of Judaism and Christianity and even collide on the pages of our Bible!"[13] Both of these images use texts from the Bible to create competing versions of God. But which is right?

"A completely free God who is pure will produces worshippers who reflect him by championing freedom at all costs. This God does whatever he pleases, even beyond good and evil. I would argue that a willful God produces willful people who ultimately do whatever they please. They will see themselves either as God's agents or, in their willfulness, reject God to become his rivals."[14]

The other primary image we form is more consistent with the theology of love we have seen. This image produces people who imitate God by exemplifying divine love. This God willingly gave up his only Son (John 3:16) for the world. God's Son laid down his life for us. "Such an

---

12. I am not suggesting that you adopt a Puritan view of Christmas and then scrub it of all festivity and joy for little children. I would rather suggest that you realize what is going on and when the time is right you teach you children that this is *not* who God is at all.

13. Jersak, *More Christlike God*, 49.

14. Jersak, *More Christlike God*, 49.

image inspires loving followers who are truly free—free to move beyond the slavery of self-seeking into self-giving, sacrificial love."[15]

Here then is the image of a Christlike God that should inform all our life.

In real life, placing freedom ahead of love actually perverts the definition of freedom. But this is what I did for years. I believed God was holy, which he clearly is. But because of God's holiness I believed he had to punish my sin retributively. I was resigned that Adam hid from God in the garden because he feared punishment. Paul said "the wages of sin is death" (Rom 6:23). I believed that. And the Bible says "we reap what we sow" (Gal 6:7–10). But we need to read these texts more carefully in their larger context. In Genesis we see that it was sin that brought death, *not God*. Genesis doesn't say that God promised to kill Adam and Eve if they ate from the forbidden tree. God said, "In the day you eat of it you will surely die." Sin caused death. God allows the judgment of love for our own good.

Does God's freedom mean we get what we want? This sounds a lot like "I am the captain of my own ship." But is this really the "freedom for which Christ set us free" (Gal 5:1)? Has this type of thinking really freed us from our crippling fears? Consider the cultural expressions of Christianity we've seen since 9/11. Does the constant cable TV news loop give us this true freedom or does it actually inspire us to a sense of anger? "While Christians once saw true freedom as a blessed byproduct of living according to virtues revealed by God, we now frequently see our freedom as living the values we create without hindrance. Jesus taught us that his truth sets us free to follow the path of love that he created. But now, Western culture defines freedom as forging one's own path, willing one's own destiny."[16]

Where love reigns God-Love will transform us by making us loving! Why? "We know love by this, that he laid down his life for us—and we ought to lay down our lives for the brothers and sisters" (1 John 3:16). Experiencing God-Love will empower you to love your neighbors (Mark 12:31). We can even learn to love our enemies (Matt 5:44). "For disciples of the Lamb, laying down our lives means laying down the sword of coercion and lethal force, and picking up the Cross of self-giving, radically forgiving love."[17] The message of God-Love never, never supports

15. Jersak, *More Christlike God*, 50.
16. Jersak, *More Christlike God*, 54.
17. Jersak, *More Christlike God*, 59.

violence as a means to the greater good. Today, more than ever, we need a nonviolent theology of love. We need to become peacemakers not warmakers. This peacemaking is never passive! It actively prays and works for the good of others.

Nothing has more radically altered my inward life than God showing me just how much he loves me by leading me to love my enemies. Why? For, "he makes his sun rise on the evil and on the good and sends rain on the righteous and on the unrighteous" (Matt 5:45). God loves his enemies! He loved us when we were his enemies. "For Christ also suffered for sins once for all, the righteous for the unrighteous" (1 Pet 3:18).

The Intimate Friendship We Have With Jesus

As Jesus was preparing his disciples for their future, after he would be raised from the dead and ascend to his Father, John records him teaching them: "I do not call you servants any longer, because the servant does not know what the master is doing, but I have called you friends" (John 15:15).

In spite of such a striking promise I do not remember ever hearing Christians speak of what we hear Jesus teach in John 15, namely that Christ calls his disciples to be his *intimate friends*. If anything our revival culture and music has no expression for this idea of real friendship with God that we saw it in chapter 10 on *abba*. The Greek word for friendship used in John 15 has a wide variety of forms that were expressed in the Greco-Roman world. Some friendships were often understood as a political alliance or a patron-client relationship. Others clearly involved personal intimacy. The latter is in view in the words in John 15.

I have always been struck by Jesus' use of this word "friends." As I engaged in research about the love of Christ I was introduced to the writing of professor Martin M. Culy. Culy says John's use of the word "friend" here conveys *intimate relationship*, rooted in what he calls "ideal friendship." "One can be a member of a family and not enjoy the level of intimacy that was characteristic of ideal friendship. The range of themes, motifs, and metaphors that are developed in the macro structure of the Fourth Gospel work together to convey a particular message—a message that highlights relational intimacy between Jesus and the Father and Jesus and his followers."[18]

---

18. Culy, *Echoes of Friendship in the Gospel of John*, 90. Culy's book is based upon

The Fourth Gospel uses this term "friends" to underscore that our relationship with God in Christ is profoundly *intimate*. "Jesus is not *like* an ideal friend to the Father; he *is* the Father's *ideal friend*. While it is generally true that discourse about God requires metaphorical language, when it comes to describing the relationship between God and Jesus both metaphorical and literal language can be employed."[19]

This friendship motif in John, and the message about the Father as our *abba* that we saw in chapter 10, both point us to a striking implication of the life, death, and resurrection of Jesus. Followers of Jesus were openly invited into true *intimacy* with Christ, *the intimacy that he enjoyed with his Father*.

I find it incredible that any of us could look at the faithfulness, kindness, and mercy of God and not be overcome with gratitude.

Is God Just?

The most consistent pushback I have faced in showing that God is love boils down to one question: "Isn't God also just?" If the very nature of God is *pure* love then have we left out the clear biblical teaching on divine justice? Dutch Reformed theologian Hendrikus Berkhof rightly argued that we cannot say God's nature is love unless we also say that God is holy. He is holy love! I agree. So let me explain.[20]

What do people mean when they speak of God's justice? Space does not allow me to show how a Western sense of justice owes more to the Greeks, the Romans, and the English court system than to the Bible. If you try to make God fit into this thinking he ultimately becomes a *divine courtroom judge*. This is, I believe, a serious misconception but one I preached for several decades. When this idea lodges in your mind and heart you will never grasp the fullness of divine love. You are not far from a series of further errors that are easily made.

So God does judge? Yes! But what kind of judge is God? Does he judge retributively, in a way that ties his hands to the *necessity* of payback? (We have already examined this in the previous chapter where we

---

his doctoral dissertation at Baylor University. I have never come across such a powerful work of scholarship with such amazing implications for the theme of love in Christ as divine friendship.

19. Culy, *Echoes of Friendship in the Gospel of John*, 91.

20. Berkhof, *Christian Faith*, 120–33. Berkhof devotes an entire section of this theology to the "Holy Love" of God.

saw how it lacks the support of Scripture.) Most of us instantly know this idea cannot be true yet we feel obliged to embrace this misconception because of what we were taught. We imagine an angry God pouring out wrath on those who disobey him. When you embrace this misconception you will read the narrative in Genesis 3 as God punishing Adam and Eve. This is also where we get the idea that Jesus died under the wrath of his Father. In this view God expresses his love only in certain ways because his justice demands payback and he has to do what justice demands since he is holy.[21]

Is this the only way to read the narrative in Genesis 3? Adam and Eve are judged by God's justice and that is the end of the story. The way I read this account sees God's justice rooted in divine grace. The goal of divine justice is to heal the victim and make offenders whole. (You can even see this in how God judges Cain for murdering his own brother.) Even the laws of the old covenant envisioned making offenders whole by providing them a way to move back into society. "[The] purpose is to put back everything that belongs. It's biblical justice that finds its course in the very heart of our triune God."[22] God-Love longs to make things right in our lives so we can live in the fullness of divine life. This understanding is not new, especially when you read the writings of the Greek-speaking church of the East.

The church father Clement of Alexandria (150–215), as just one example, said that "as children are chastened by the teacher or their father so are we by Providence . . . [for] God does not take vengeance (for vengeance is a retaliation of evil), but he chastens with a view to the good."[23] The previously mentioned Isaac the Syrian (613–700) was convinced that God's fundamental motivation for creating and overseeing the affairs of humans was that of love. "Among all [God's] actions there is none which is not entirely a matter of mercy, love, and compassion: this constitutes the beginning and the end of his dealings with us."[24]

To put this very simply I now argue that most of our religious conflict boils down to one issue—is God truly and always loving? Are we warranted to view God as a loving father? If so should then we not view the real purpose of his punishment as "perfect fatherly love?"[25]

21. McVey, *Beyond an Angry God*, 77–94.
22. McVey, *Beyond an Angry God*, 81.
23. Clement of Alexandria, *Miscellanies Book VII*, 16.102, 181.
24. Isaac the Syrian, *Second Part*, 39.15, 170.
25. Wessling, *Love Divine*, 32.

Amazing Grace

The best known hymn in all the world is undoubtedly John Newton's *Amazing Grace*. It is sung in cathedrals and country churches, in simple non-creedal Protestant churches, as well as in Catholic masses around the world. It is not surprising that this simple hymn is so popular. But what really is *amazing* about grace? I believe we can rightly say that grace is the one biblical word that truly defines our relationship with God. But how does grace relate to the theology of God-Love?

> The theology of grace is in the main the theology of God's love for us and of the love which God's first love has caused in us. Viewed from God's side, grace signifies first and foremost the wealth and majesty of God's love which enfolds us all in one gesture and, at the same time speaks to each of us in accordance with our most intimate dispositions and, so to say, from within the individual situation in life particularly our own.... Viewed from man's side, grace signifies rebirth in Christ. It denotes a mysterious but nonetheless eminently real stream of life which wells up from the deepest stratum of our being where it rests securely in the creative hand of God.[26]

Behold the Glory of the Lord

Paul says we grasp "the glory of the Lord" by embracing the One who loves us. The real question has never been "Do you believe the right things taught in the Bible?" It is this: "Has the Spirit removed the veil which covers your eyes?" That which is veiled to our inner eyes is the glory of the Lord, thus Paul says, "When one turns to the Lord, the veil is removed" (2 Cor 4:6). Moses said the glory of the Lord is God's "goodness," which is a way of saying "the character of God" (cf. Exod 33:18–19). This glory of God's goodness is what we've called God-Love. The First Epistle of John gives us a marvelous account of what happens when we see God's character as perfect love (1 John 3:1–3).

We are thus brought full circle. The various misconceptions of God that hinder our understanding of divine love must fall away. But how? When we know God's grace and see the glory of the Lord, we will see God's perfectly holy character revealed as inexhaustibly perfect love. *Then we will begin to be like him.* This is the eternal hope that purifies us.

26. Franzen, *New Life of Grace*, 1.

If we walk by faith in God-Love then we are being transformed moment by moment into this life of divine love. This is the gospel Paul preached, which can be seen in his words to the first-century Roman Christians: "Owe no one anything, except to love one another, for the one who loves another has *fulfilled the law*" (Rom 13:8).

Will This Understanding of God-Love Lead Us Astray?

Many Christians, as I have noted several times, believe my understanding of God-Love will lead us astray. Are they right? Obviously I do not believe this is the case. But not only is it possible for this to be true, I believe the way love has been *misused* has led many astray. The enemy does not much care what imbalance traps us. We must grasp "God is love" rightly, seeing it as the expression of who God is in his character—the *totality* of his infinite being, goodness, and wisdom. For this to be true we must clear the ground of sentimental and self-serving projections. We must find ourselves in complete awe of the God who desires us *because* he is love.

Theologian Anthony J. Kelly underscores the two sides of this possible imbalance as well as any writer I have read. This long quotation sums up beautifully my own understanding.

> The recognition of the particularity in time and space of God's self-revelation in Christ originally provoked the amazement expressed in the phrase "God is Love." Yet it is an amazement born out of awe. The infinite God, the God of limitless goodness and beauty, of power and intelligence, the creator of all that is, the One in whom "we live and move and have our being" (Acts 17: 28), has shown himself in such a way as to be named as "Love." The wonder of God's love can never be exhausted. True, a certain kind of emotionally repressive fixation can occur when all the emphasis falls on the idea of love in a monodimensional way. It is suspiciously close to a self-regarding human projection, basically unaware of God's sheer initiative. In other words, this most radical biblical sentence can be reduced to meaning "love is God." A superficial sentimentality can take over—romantic at best, self-serving at worst. When the awe-inspiring transcendence of God is swallowed up into mere sentiment, a growing caution marks the interpretation of this biblical phrase.[27]

---

27. Kelly, *God Is Love*, 112.

To avoid this imbalance in our thinking and living we must adopt the *full biblical vocabulary of divine love* and keep these truths always in mind. The profound theological significance of God-Love must reach into our innermost being. I have written with the prayerful hope that this book will help you do this with all your heart, mind, soul, and strength (cf. Mark 12:30; Luke 10:27).

Chapter Fifteen

Can We Experience God's Love?

> But there are not a few who would be indignant
> at having their belief in God questioned, who yet
> seem to fear imagining Him better than He is.
> —George MacDonald

> There will never be beings unloved by
> God, since God is absolute love.
> —Hans Urs von Balthasar

> Thirst after Jesus and he will satisfy you with his love.
> —Isaac the Syrian

THE FAMOUS ANGLICAN ARCHBISHOP Desmond Tutu, winner of the 1984 Nobel Peace Prize, was a remarkable person. He made it his constant goal to *live* his life in the love of God. Tutu once referred to how those who worked with him for spiritual and social reformation in South Africa understood God's presence in their labors.

It was all happening because God is good and loving—loving us prodigally and without limit. All we were and all we had were gifts, bestowed freely without measure. All we would become was a response to this prevenient love and prodigal grace. We would become good because we were loved, and loved, and will be loved forever and ever.[1]

Desmond Tutu's sense of being "loved forever and ever" has become my experience. But as you've seen, this was not the case for years. I was an actively sought-after speaker and Christian mentor but I had not yet learned how to live in the abiding joy of God-Love. While I can never remember not believing in God, what I knew about God I primarily learned through ideas that were shaped by an amalgam of prooftexts and popular misconceptions. Of course, I knew the Bible verses on love that we've seen. I obviously knew transformative love was real but I had no idea how or why.

As I said at the beginning, growing up in Christianity I do not remember any clear teaching on the *nature* of God as love. This profound truth was treated like a hackneyed phrase or listed as one of several divine attributes. For these, and countless other reasons, the truth of God-Love did not empower me. Honestly, I was sometimes terrified by my thoughts of God, especially by my thoughts of his almighty power and intense hatred of sin. I believe my deepest desire was to please God but this desire did not lead me into a deep *experience* of love. When I began to ask why, my world slowly changed.

After fifty-plus years of ministry, in multiple church contexts and countries, and through an intensely personal ecumenical dialogue with all of the great Christian traditions—Catholic, Protestant, and Orthodox—I submit that there are many types of unhealthy spirituality that we commonly experience. The reasons for this vary.

Through an emphasis on God's hatred of sin, and the need to turn from his wrath against me, I learned the idea of penal substation that I addressed earlier. I saw Jesus' death as the means for placating the Father's anger. The gospel became a message about Jesus dying in my place so that the Father could forgive me, since Jesus "paid it all." This gospel was more of a transaction with a courtroom judge than an encounter with God-Love. It was a set of beliefs about Christ and the cross and a particular view of the atonement. I believed Christ died for me and I

---

1. Borg and Mackenzie, eds., *God at 2000*, 177.

accepted God's gift. Yet I often felt paralyzed and did not know what to do with my unsettled inner self.

So can we embrace God as love without falling into the common binary choices of conservative or liberal Christianity? I believe so. To my mind these categories, as they are widely and popularly used today, have outlived their usefulness. "The critical division now is between those who commit themselves to live deeply from the center and those who are superficial, who float free, unanchored in any depth."[2]

Can We *Experience* God's Love?

In my growing desire for the experience of divine love I discovered authors, both ancient and modern, who provided answers to the questions I was asking. But I needed more than answers. I needed life in the Spirit. I needed to *experience* the all-consuming love of God. I needed both internal and external transformation. One author who helped me move into this experience was the British Jesuit Gerard W. Hughes (1924–2014). In 1985 Hughes wrote an amazing book, *God of Surprises*. (This book became a spiritual classic.)[3] Eugene H. Peterson wrote the foreword to the third American edition of *God of Surprises*. In the preface Hughes said he experienced a "powerful in-breaking of the God of surprises, truths of a Christian faith with which I was familiarly bored, or doubted, [which] began to take on new meaning." These words summarized my life until I came into the experience of God-Love. I am persuaded they describe the path followed by way too many Christians. This truth of divine love was just an attribute in a list. It did nothing to profoundly transform most of us. Hughes wrote what I experienced: "As God breaks down the cocoon of our closed minds, God enters it, no longer remote, and out there, no longer dwelling only in tabernacles and temples of stone, but we meet God smiling at us in our bewilderment, beckoning to us in our confusion and revealing Godself in our failure and disillusion as our only rock, refuge and strength."[4]

It seems apparent to me that our minds contain something like layers of consciousness. Growth requires breaking into new layers,

---

2. Kelly, *God Is Love*, 115.

3. Hughes, *God of Surprises*. Over 250,000 copies of the book have been sold worldwide. The book has been translated into over twenty languages. Like me, Hughes came to the questions by working in ecumenism.

4. Hughes, *God of Surprises*, xvi.

Can We Experience God's Love?

something we naturally fear. Why? We fear what we do not know. Our journey through these layers "will always be accompanied by some measure of uncertainty, pain and confusion. I believe these negative feelings are the nudging of God. The facts are kind, and God is in the facts."[5] Remember, Jesus said: "The kingdom of heaven is like treasure hidden in a field, which a man found and reburied; then in his joy he goes and sells all that he has and buys that field" (Matt 13:44). Breaking through to the transforming presence of God-Love will always require effort, the kind of effort we see in buying a field to search and dig for treasure!

Eventually I learned how to experience love as *the* most powerful reality in all the world. Looking back I realize now that the more I actually read the New Testament—especially using ancient methods of listening to the text like *lectio divina*[6]—the more I came into the experience of divine love. What I learned was how to search for this great mystery that I found continually enlightening my true self. Love shone through biblical texts like never before. (Sometimes this came through one single word I would meditate upon for the day.)

On virtually every page of the four Gospels we encounter enigmatic events and statements. After two thousand years of Scripture study we seem to have just begun to see what was already there. I think it is safe to say that the Gospels are awash with this mystery of love. At the heart of these mysteries are the central truths we have considered in this book—truths such as the nature of faith, the meaning of divine love and the being of God as both transcendent and immanent.

The great tradition of the Western church deeply pondered these particular questions in the thirteenth century. Some concluded that believers were called to live a radical "unknowing." But the church forgot this call, opting instead to protect itself from such liberating insights. Why? The real truth of divine love goes against everything we think religion should be about. Nothing seems to confuse people like talking of "unknowing." This means we surrender our cherished insights and egos and allow God's love to overwhelm us. We daily ask God to reveal himself to us. We learn to listen, not just talk. To know from the heart, personally

---

5. Hughes, *God of Surprises*, xvi.

6. *Lectio Divina* is a method of Bible reading that begins with reading the text slowly. One is encouraged to use their imagination in hearing the text and in listening for "the still, small voice." In this way God is teaching us to listen and to seek him in silence. The reader then takes a single word (maybe a short phrase) and ponders this. Finally the method leads to prayer.

and profoundly, we must learn to "unknow" the ways we have allowed our thoughts to seek concepts rather than to hear God speak. The unnamed author of the classic *The Cloud of Unknowing* put this well.

> God can well be loved, but he cannot be thought. By love he can be grasped and held, but by thought, neither grasped nor held. And therefore, though it may be good at times to think specifically of the kindness and excellence of God, and though this may be a light and a part of contemplation, all the same, in the work of contemplation itself, it must be cast down and covered with a cloud of forgetting.[7]

This is one way the contemplative tradition came to know what we earlier called the true self. All of this might seem exaggerated, yet St. Catherine of Genoa—a married woman, a mystic, and a Catholic saint—put this in a way that, at least at first, seemed totally exaggerated to me. "My God is me, nor do I recognize any other me except my God. Godself."[8]

Given the ever-present dangers of self-worship, Catherine's statement sounds heretical to modern American Christians. But I see in her words that God is *transforming* me into the very *image* of Christ.[9] (I never deeply understood this idea either.) Kallistos Ware said what I now understand: "As Christians we affirm not pantheism but 'panentheism.' God is in all things yet also beyond and above all things. He is both 'greater than great' and 'smaller than the small.' In the words of St. Gregory Palamas, 'He is everywhere and nowhere, he is everything and he is nothing.'"[10] This is the profound way the church embraced God's transcendence and immanence.

This Is My Father's World

When I was a pastor I taught our church family to learn and sing a "hymn of the month." This practice stocked my mind and heart with the poetry

---

7. Walsh, ed., *Cloud of Unknowing*.
8. Hughes, *God of Surprises*, ix.
9. Panentheism means "all in God." Unlike pantheism, which holds that the divine and the universe are identical, panentheism maintains an ontological distinction between the divine and the non-divine and the deep significance of both.
10. Ware, *Orthodox Way*, 48.

of faith and a growing desire to know God. One hymn we learned together said:

> This is my Father's world:
> The birds their carol raise,
> The morning light, the lily white,
> Declare their Maker's praise.
> This is my Father's world:
> He shines in all that's fair;
> In rustling grass I hear him pass,
> He speaks to me everywhere.[11]

Consider this truth—*God really is in all things and God really does speak to me everywhere and in all things. I must, however, learn to listen. This will take a lifetime.*

This world in which we live is our Father's world. When we begin to contemplate God's presence as love, something life-transforming happens. We see God's immanence in his glorious creation. Like Moses we need to "take off our shoes," recognizing that we stand on holy ground.[12] Augustine said God is "*intimior intimo meo*—closer to me than I am to myself."[13] Many early Christian theologians actually spoke of creation as a sacrament, a sign of God's presence. But our underdeveloped spirituality tends to focus only on God's transcendence to the exclusion of his immanence. "We would prefer God either to be transcendent or to be immanent. We can manage one, or the other: we find both to be unmanageable. The truth of the matter is that we are unable to 'manage' God despite our best endeavors. We have to surrender, and if we fail to do so it is not possible for God to be God to us and through us."[14]

St. Thomas Aquinas, writing in the thirteenth century, said everything we understand comes to us through our senses. What he meant was this: we can only come to a knowledge of God through our sense experience of God's creation and the love of Christ. This means that if we try to know God by ignoring our experience we will end up with an abstraction. God must, in some way, be *within us* if our ultimate identity is to be found. We are called to be at one with God right now, not just in the future after our death. Our very hunger for the knowledge and truth

---

11. Maltbie D. Babcock (1858–1901), "This Is My Father's World."

12. I love the fact that in many cultures where I have ministered Christians remove their shoes when they enter into public worship.

13. Augustine, *Confessions*, 3.6.11.

14. Hughes, *God of Surprises*, 20.

of God is a mark of this divine transcendence. And this transcendence lies at the heart of all true religion.

I also understand that the most significant sign of God's transcendence is his presence *within* us. St. Augustine famously said, "God, you have created me for yourself, and my heart is restless until it rests in you."[15] When we ask ourselves what we most desire we begin to understand the meaning of divine transcendence. We see that no thing/nothing can ever completely satisfy our innate hunger. Our human limitations are so profoundly real that when we cease to dream we cease to hunger for God. Love takes us out of ourselves to the deepest place where our inner self is transformed by God-Love. This can be seen in one of the most enigmatic sayings of Jesus in which he called us to lose our life in order to find it (Matt 10:39). The truth of these words can be seen in what happens when we surrender our self-centeredness and begin to serve others freely. Furthermore our desire for transcendence underscores that our deepest desire, in itself, is *not* a bad thing. The problem is *what* we desire. We need to learn to situate our desire in the life and love of Christ.

A Prayer: Open the Eyes of My Heart

Opening ourselves up to the mystery of God is the first step in real spiritual and emotional growth. If you are to enter into the fullness of Christ you must take deliberate steps of faith every day. Paul expressed the comprehension of the love of Christ in his Epistle to the Ephesians (3:18–19). "I pray that you may have the power to comprehend, with all the saints, what is the breadth and length and height and depth and *to know the love of Christ that surpasses knowledge, so that you may be filled with all the fullness of God*" (italics underscore the point I am making here.)

There is no way to read such words without concluding that we are invited by the Spirit into this *transformational knowing of the love of Christ through union with Christ*. The Eastern Church theologians called this "deification," or *participation* in the divine nature (2 Pet 1:4). *God is transforming us by our participation in the life of the Father, Son, and Holy Spirit.*

The process of being filled with the fullness of God reaches its intended purpose when we become our "true self," which is the person God created us to be. This is the human person being transformed into the mystery of Christ.

---

15. Augustine, *Confessions*, 1.1.1.

> My beloved friends, let us continue to love each other since love comes from God. *Everyone who loves is born of God and experiences a relationship with God.* The person who refuses to love doesn't know the first thing about God, because God *is* love—so you can't know him if you don't love." (1 John 4:7–8, *MSG*).

When you are born of God's Spirit life takes on a whole new meaning. Indeed, for most people this is a total life-change, a new beginning. Paul puts it this way: "So if anyone is in Christ, there is a new creation: everything old has passed away" (2 Cor 5:17).

It was said that Martin Luther, towards the end of his life, said, "God has led me like a blind horse." All thoughtful people know something of Luther's experience. God's ways often seem roundabout. In a sense the journey of Israel out of bondage from Egypt to Canaan is a paradigm of every spiritual journey we embark upon. This is the "model story" for living faith! We are tempted to think God's ways are foolish. But when you seek God you will soon learn that your ways are not nearly as wise as you thought. God's ways are always better.

Our Eternal Future Is Love

We can now begin to imagine what our future might be like when we are among the saints and angels in heaven. But the great twentieth-century theologian Karl Rahner has given us an important caution here. "It is a priori senseless to ask where Heaven is, if by this 'where' we are to understand location in our physical, spatial world."[16]

I heard a popular saying in my teen years that I have never forgotten. More than a few minsters would say: "Don't become so heavenly minded that you are no earthly good." I now realize how wrong this counsel was. If you draw every breath you take from the God of love then you are literally praying heavenly prayers, in union with Christ. This is what praying without ceasing really means (cf. 1 Thess 5:17). This reality had a huge impact on how Christians learned to live Trinity-Love in the first centuries of the church. You will seek to give God more glory when you move "out of your self-centeredness, and move yourself into the burning bush of God's triune presence within you and within each creature that you encounter."[17]

---

16. Rahner, *Theological Investigations: Confrontations*, 215.
17. Maloney, *Abiding in the Indwelling Trinity*, 149.

Perhaps you are thinking, at this point, that this all sounds like self-centeredness. But Fr. George Maloney puts this so powerfully when he says we can touch the heart of the cosmic Christ in love but only as we live in the depths of our true being, in our hearts. "How deeply your heart has entered into the heart of Christ and how much of God's fire of love you have allowed to touch yourself are measured by how much fiery love you show in service to others."[18] This is the only way to real transformation.

How to Proceed

There are almost as many ways to proceed into knowing and experiencing God-Love as there are people. No one way works for all of us. I began to pray "the Jesus Prayer" many years ago and it has continued to help me a great deal. This simple prayer says: "Lord Jesus Christ, Son of God, have mercy on me a sinner." It is rooted in Luke 23:34. (There is a marvelous short article on this prayer on a seminary website.)[19]

I mentioned earlier that I also adopted Brennan Manning's simple prayer: "Abba, I belong to you!" This can be prayed, like the Jesus Prayer, throughout the day. It reminds me of what we saw in our chapter on "Abba," about the intimate, tender, and fatherly love of God.

I agree with many teachers that each of us needs a spiritual theology that works for us. Centering prayer has become such a resource for some. Different types of meditative practice benefit many Christians. One thing is certain, find ways to be reminded by your experience that the awesome and infinite God revealed in Scripture desires to daily reveal his love to you.

Robert J. Wicks, a Catholic spiritual theologian and trained counselor, suggests that we need a personal spiritual theology. He uses questions to help us find our own way to love. Some of these are:

1. When I think of God what images flash into my mind?

2. Given these images, what do I expect of God when I become depressed, stressful, confused, lost, frightened, angry, or worried?

3. If I were to describe God to my closest friend what would I say?

4. What difference does my personal relationship with God make in my day-to-day life?

---

18. Maloney, *Abiding in the Indwelling Trinity*, 150.
19. https://www.svots.edu/saying-jesus-prayer.

5. What affective interpersonal style was present in my family? Were people physically demonstrative in their love? In their anger? Who in my family am I most like in relating to others?
6. What do I really believe God thinks of me?
7. How can I begin to see myself as God sees me?
8. With whom in my life do I relate to most closely to the way in which I relate to God?
9. What word best describes my relationship with God?[20]

I could list more but you get the idea. Learn to develop a spiritual theology that works for you in knowing and experiencing divine love.

Where Is Your Treasure?

The Scripture plainly teaches that God has chosen to reveal himself to us through divine revelation.[21] When we say God is revealed we must understand that we are referring to the mystery of his presence unveiled in history (John 9:5). Augustine said that through this revelation God's redemptive purpose was made known. John Calvin even said that the shock waves from the center resound in the farthest reaches of the cosmos.[22]

I maintain that the unveiling of this divine mystery ultimately shows us that God is love. This is how the Scripture becomes *our* love story!

One Modern Movement of Love

As South Africa faced the social and spiritual blight of apartheid, a profound struggle to end it emerged. As I noted earlier, this movement was primarily the work of Christians who had experienced divine love. Their actions made a huge difference while the country teetered on the brink of prolonged violence. Archbishop Desmond Tutu recounts what then happened.

---

20. Wicks, *Seeds of Sensitivity*, 132–33.
21. The word "revelation" here unites two biblical words: (1) The idea of unveiling (*apocalypses*), which means disclosure or coming, and (2) the idea of making known (*phanerōsis*), which means manifesting or expressing.
22. Calvin, *Institutes of the Christian Religion*, 1–6.

Ultimately, even our prayer life changed. We would become less active, less talkative, and more contemplative. We did not seek to prove ourselves, or justify our existence, or try to impress God. We learned just to be, to be silent, to be quiet in the presence of the mystery that is God, for whom all language is ultimately so utterly inadequate. We learned just to be there, and hear the Psalmist say, "Open your mouth wide and I will fill it" (Psalm 81:10). "My soul waits in silence; from him comes my salvation" (Psalm 62:1). "Be still, and know that I am God" (Psalm 46:10). Just be there![23]

Just be there. Why? Because God is eternally love!

The experience of God-Love can move mountains, change nations, and renew the church.

This is *the* message of the Bible. Any other message distorts the love of God revealed in Jesus Christ and hinders true spiritual renewal. Our hearts hunger for this love, this treasure that *abba* puts in our inner being. Our inner life directly affects our perceptions of the world and determines our every action and reaction to it. But in our busyness we tend to ignore the inner life.

The image I have before me at the end of my writing is one of sitting in front of a fire, not a fire that will destroy me but one that will warm and transform me. As with the fire Moses encountered in the burning bush this fire will not consume me. This fire is love! I need do nothing to receive the grace of this fire. I just need to be present.

God loves you. In fact, he loves you immensely. He really does. Begin to believe this truth and seek to intentionally live it moment by moment. Rest in God's love and know that this alone creates real life. "This discovery of Love, the acceptance in ourselves of infinite Love will be a new creation. At every moment, Love wants to create amongst you yet more love."[24]

Why I Write

I must be honest. On one level I had little reason to write this book, yet it has occupied my mind and heart for many years. I promise you I have said nothing truly *new!* What I have written has been believed and written by countless others. (My copious footnotes demonstrate this point.)

---

23. Borg and Mackenzie, eds., *God at 2000*, 177.
24. Gillet, *In Thy Presence*, 13.

What I have tried to do is *listen* attentively to both the Scripture and the living Christian tradition, all of it. What I have written might help you if you learn to "unknow" and listen.

The mystery we've seen is infinite and inexhaustible. We will never solve this mystery, even in the age to come. In fact, it is not something to be solved. To stop and say "It is enough, I now know all I need to know" is never possible. St. Irenaeus said, "God will always have something more to teach man, and man will always have something more to learn from God." This does not mean we are strangers and exiles from the presence of God. It means that the way of faith lies beyond our words and thoughts, something our age has a profound problem with.

St. Athanasius famously said in *On the Incarnation*: "For the Son of God became man so that man might become God." (St. Irenaeus said virtually the same thing before Athanasius.) This was a common idea in the early church. In uniting God's nature with our human nature God raised up our human nature. Because God became human, humans can now partake of God's divine nature—not becoming God but by being divinized. We share such an intimate communion with God that we can be transformed. But when I search online sites about this famous statement I encounter comments like this: "This doesn't make much sense to me. I don't think God is just controlling a human body like an avatar. I don't understand why/how this individual transformation would necessarily mean that humanity as a whole is changed, too." Indeed, this person does not understand what we've seen about God and his transforming work.

So why do I feel compelled to write a book about my journey to divine love? I do it for two reasons. First, it helps me to go deeper into my own experience of God's love by writing. (It has been said that writing makes an "exact man.") Second, I sincerely hope I have helped you to begin this journey.

It took me many years to find the truths that compelled me to finish this book. Several of my best friends encouraged me to share my story in my own voice. In effect, their gentle arguments convinced me that I did have a message about God-Love. Some may find things I've said new, even strange. I hope you will finally see that this is a message that is nothing less than ancient, mainstream, and orthodox Christian faith. With the whole church I gladly affirm the historic ecumenical creeds and follow Christ as my Lord.

Therefore my hope is simple: *I desire that you understand and experience how vast and deep is the love of God.* I pray you will grasp that the

Christian answer to the question "Who is God?" will always be incomplete without this statement, "God is love" (1 John 4:8, 16). I pray you will be enabled by the Spirit to see how the Christian faith embraces the fullness of God, a fullness revealed in God-Love seen in Jesus Christ. This love is so wonderful that a nineteenth-century hymn, sung for decades as a solo by the great George Beverly Shea at the Billy Graham evangelistic meetings, says it almost perfectly.

> The love of God is greater far
> than tongue or pen can ever tell;
> it goes beyond the highest star,
> and reaches to the lowest hell.
>
> The wandering child is reconciled
> by God's beloved Son.
> The aching soul again made whole,
> and priceless pardon won.
>
> When ancient time shall pass away,
> and human thrones and kingdoms fall;
> when those who here refuse to pray
> on rocks and hills and mountains call;
>
> God's love so sure, shall still endure,
> all measureless and strong;
> grace will resound the whole earth round—
> the saints' and angels' song. [Refrain]
>
> Could we with ink the ocean fill,
> and were the skies of parchment made;
> were ev'ry stalk on earth a quill,
> and everyone a scribe by trade;
>
> To write the love of God above
> would drain the ocean dry;
> nor could the scroll contain the whole,
> though stretched from sky to sky.
>
> Refrain:
> O love of God, how rich and pure!
> How measureless and strong!
> It shall forevermore endure—
> the saints' and angels' song.[25]

---

25. "The Love of God" (1917), Frederick M. Lehman.

Postscript

THE WEEK I FINISHED writing this book a dear friend shared a moving story with me that underscored the power of divine love. I believe it provides a fitting postscript.

My friend works alongside a gifted and highly educated man with whom he had been conversing about faith in Christ for more than fifteen years. Unprompted by any recent conversation or discussion of the things of Christ (in fact, there had been no spiritual discussions for months) his friend walked into his office one morning and said, "I encountered the most amazing thing this morning on my way to work. I stopped for gasoline and saw a sign at the station that said, 'God Loves You.' I thought to myself, 'He really does love me.' And then, within minutes, I saw a truck where someone had written in the dust on the side of the truck, 'God Loves You.' I was melted by this truth." Then my friend asked him if maybe this was the time he should answer the question; you know, the question that Jesus is really asking when he leans into a person by the power of the Spirit and says to his lost son "Follow me." His friend responded through tears, "I think I already have. I think this is why those words (God is love) have overwhelmed me so!"

The kairos moment had come for this man. When he saw that God really loved him he was ready to fully and completely trust Christ.

I pray that you, my reader, will embrace this message of divine love as your kairos moment.

Bibliography

Alfayev, Metropolitan Hilarion. *The Mystery of Faith: An Introduction to the Teaching and Spirituality of the Orthodox Church*. Crestwood, NY: St. Vladimir's Seminary Press, 2011.
———. *The Spiritual World of Isaac the Syrian*. Collegeville, MN: Liturgical, 2000.
Andreopoulos, Andreas. *This Is My Beloved Son*. Brewster, MA: Paraclete, 2012.
Armstrong, John H. *Costly Love: The Way of True Unity for All the Followers of Jesus*. Hyde Park, NY: New City, 2017.
———. *True Revival: What Happens When God's Spirit Moves*. Eugene, OR: Harvest House, 2001.
Augustine, Saint. *Confessions*. Translated by Henry Chadwick. Oxford: Oxford University Press, 1992.
Balthasar, Hans Urs Von. *Dare We Hope That All Men Will Be Saved?* San Francisco: Ignatius, 2014.
———. *Love Alone is Credible*. San Francisco: Ignatius, 2004.
Baima, Thomas. "Christianity: Origins and Beliefs." March, 2015. https://parliamentofreligions.org/content/christianity-origins-and-beliefs.
Barth, Karl. *Church Dogmatics*. Edited and translated by G. W. Bromiley et al. Edinburgh: T. & T. Clark, 1969–1975.
Bartos, Emil. *Deification in Eastern Theology*. Waynesboro, GA: Paternoster, 1999.
Benson, George. *The Silent Self: A Journey of Spiritual Discovery*. Cincinnati: Forward Movement, 1992.
Berkhof, Hendrikus. *Christian Faith: An Introduction to the Study of Faith*. Translated by Sierd Woudstra. Grand Rapids: Eerdmans, 1979.
Bloesch, Donald G. *God the Almighty: Power, Wisdom, Holiness, Love*. Christian Foundations. Downers Grove, IL: InterVarsity, 1995.
Borg, Marcus, and Ross Mackenzie, eds. *God at 2000*. New York: Moorehouse, 2000.
Bouyer, Louis. *Dictionary of Theology*. Tournai, Belgium (English edition, 1965).
Bread and Wine: Readings for Lent and Easter. Farmington, PA: Plough, 2003.
Brown, Raymond E. *The Gospel of John, I–XII*. Anchor Bible. New York: Doubleday, 1966.
Brunner, Emil. *The Mediator: A Study of the Central Doctrine of the Christian Faith*. Philadelphia: Westminster, 1947.
Buechner, Frederick. *The Clown in the Belfry: Writings on Faith and Fiction*. San Francisco: Harper, 1992.

Bibliography

Caba, José. "Abba Father." In *Dictionary of Fundamental Theology*, edited by René Latourelle and Rino Fisichella, 1–3. New York: Crossroad, 1994.

Calvin, John. *Institutes of the Christian Religion*. Louisville: Westminster John Knox Press, 1960.

Campbell, Douglas A. *Pauline Dogmatics: The Triumph of God's Love*. Grand Rapids: Eerdmans, 2020.

Carson, Donald A. *The Difficult Doctrine of the Love of God*. Wheaton, IL: Crossway, 2000.

Cerini, Marisa. *God Who Is Love in the Experience and Thought of Chiara Lubich*. Hyde Park, NY: New City, 1992.

Chartier, Gary. *The Analogy of Love: Divine and Human Love at the Center of Christian Theology*. 2nd ed. Ann Arbor, MI: Griffin & Lash, 2017.

Clasper, Paul. *Eastern Paths and the Christian Way*. Maryknoll, NY: Orbis, 1980.

Clement of Alexandria. *Miscellanies Book VII*. Translated by Fenton Anthony Sort. Cambridge: Cambridge University Press, 2010.

Clements, Richard. *The Meaning of the World is Love: Selected Texts from Hans Urs von Balthasar*. San Francisco: Ignatius, 2022.

Cobb, John B., Jr. *Jesus' Abba: The God Who Has Not Failed*. Minneapolis: Fortress, 2015.

Culy, Martin M. *Echoes of Friendship in the Gospel of John*. Sheffield: Sheffield Phoenix, 2010.

Des Places, Edouard. "Platonism and Christianity." In *Dictionary of Fundamental Theology*, edited by René Latourelle and Rino Fisichella, 781. New York: Crossroad, 1994.

Earle, Mary C. *Julian of Norwich: Selections from Revelations of Divine Love—Annotated & Explained*. Woodstock, VT: Skylight Paths, 2013.

Edwards, Jonathan. *Charity and Its Fruits: The Works of Jonathan Edwards*. Vol. 8. Edited by Paul Ramsey. New Haven: Yale University Press, 1989.

Evely, Louis. *Credo*. Notre Dame: Fides, 1967.

———. *Rejoice! Gospel Mediations*. New York: Doubleday, 1974.

———. *A Religion for Our Time*. New York: Herder & Herder, 1968.

Ford, David F., and Mike Higton, eds. *Jesus*. New York: Oxford University Press, 2002.

Foster, Richard J. *Prayer: Finding the Heart's True Home*. San Francisco: HarperOne, 1992.

Francis, Pope. "The Way of the Cross." Catholic Insight. http://catholicinsight.com/the-way-of-the-cross.

Franzen, Peter. *The New Life of Grace*. Tournai, Belgium: Desclee, 1969.

Freeman, Stephen. *Every Where Present: Christianity in a One-Storey Universe*. Chesterton, IN: Ancient Faith, 2010.

Freeman, Stephen. "Alone—You Are Not." In a blog at https://glory2godforallthings.com/2023/10/28/alone-you-are-not-2/.

Fretheim, Terence E. *God So Enters Into Relationships That . . . A Biblical View*. Minneapolis: Fortress, 2020.

———. *The Suffering of God: An Old Testament Perspective*. Philadelphia: Fortress, 1984.

George, Timothy. "No Squishy Love," Parts 1 and 2. *First Things*, July 29 and August 26, 2013. https://www.firstthings.com/web-exclusives/2013/07/no-squishy-love (Part One), and https://www.firstthings.com/web-exclusives/2013/08/no-squishy-love-part-ii (Part Two).

Bibliography

Gibson, Ty. *An Endless Falling in Love*. Nampa, ID: Pacific, 2003.
Gillet, Lev. *The Burning Bush*. Springfield, IL: Template, 1976.
———. *In Thy Presence*. Crestwood, NY: St. Vladimir's Seminary Press, 1977.
Gilson, Étienne. *The Mystical Theology of St. Bernard*. New York: Sheed & Ward, 1940.
The Glenstal Book of Readings for the Seasons. Dublin: Columba, 2008.
Grenz, Stanley J. *Theology for the Community of God*. Nashville: Broadman & Holman, 1994.
Groves, Peter. *Grace: The Cruciform Love of God*. London: Canterbury, 2012.
Gunton, Colin. *The Actuality of the Atonement*. Edinburgh: T. & T. Clark, 1988.
Guroian, Vigen. *The Melody of Faith: Theology in an Orthodox Key*. Grand Rapids: Eerdmans, 2010.
———. *The Orthodox Reality: Culture, Theology, and Ethics in the Modern World*. Grand Rapids: Eerdmans, 2018.
Hamilton, Adam. *Creed: What Christians Believe and Why*. Nashville: Abingdon, 2016.
Hughes, Gerard W. *God of Surprises*. Grand Rapids: Eerdmans, 1985.
Irenaeus. *The Demonstration of the Apostolic Preaching 12*. Translated by Armitage Robinson. London: SPCK, 1920.
Isaac the Syrian. *Isaac of Nineveh (Isaac the Syrian), The Second Part, Chapters IV–XLI*. Translated by Sebastian P. Brock. Louvain: Peeters, 1995.
Jacobson, Rolf A., ed. *Crazy Talk: A Not-So-Stuffy Dictionary of Theological Terms*. Minneapolis: Augsburg, 2008.
Jeremiah, David. *God Loves You: He Always Has—He Always Will*. New York: Hachette, 2012.
Jeremias, Joachim. *The Central Message of the New Testament*. London: SCM, 1955.
Jersak, Bradley. *A More Christlike God: A More Beautiful Gospel*. Pasadena, CA: Plain Truth Ministries, 2013.
Julian of Norwich. *Julian of Norwich: Selections from* Revelations of Divine Love— *Annotated and Explained*. Annotated by Mary C. Earle. SkyLight Illuminations. Woodstock, VT: SkyLight Paths, 2013.
Kelly, Anthony J. *God Is Love: The Heart of Christian Faith*. Collegeville, MN: Liturgical, 2012.
Kreeft, Peter. *The God Who Loves You*. San Francisco: Ignatius, 1988.
Küng, Hans. *On Being a Christian*. New York: Doubleday, 1976.
Latourelle, René and Rino Fisichella, eds. *Dictionary of Fundamental Theology*. Crossroads: New York, 1994.
LaVerdiere, Eugene. *The Beginning of the Gospel*. Vol. 2. Collegeville, MN: Liturgical, 1999.
Lewis, C. S. *The Four Loves*. London: Geoffrey Bles, 1960.
Lindberg, Carter. *Love: A Brief History Through Western Christianity*. Malden, MA: Blackwell, 2008.
Lucado, Max. *3:16: The Numbers of Hope*. Nashville: Thomas Nelson, 2007.
———. *Walking with the Savior*. Wheaton, IL: Tyndale, 1993.
MacGregor, Geddes. *He Who Lets Us Be: A Theology of Love*. New York: Seabury, 1975.
Maloney, George A. *Abiding in the Indwelling Trinity*. Mahwah, NJ: Paulist, 2004.
———. *God's Community of Love: Living in the Indwelling Trinity*. Hyde Park, NY: New City, 1993.
Manning, Brennan. *The Ragamuffin Gospel*. Colorado Springs: Multnomah, 1990.
———. *Ruthless Trust*. New York: Harper, 2000.

Matthews, Thomas. *Under the Influence*. New York: Macmillan, 1977.
McVey, Steve. *Beyond an Angry God*. Eugene, OR: Harvest House, 2014.
Migliore, Daniel L. *Faith Seeking Understanding: An Introduction to Christian Theology*. 3rd ed. Grand Rapids, 2014.
Mitchell, Don, ed. *Paradise: Reflections on Chiara Lubich's Mystical Journey*. Hyde Park, NY: New City, 2020.
Moltmann, Jürgen. *God in Creation: A New Theology of Creation and the Spirit of God*. London: SCM, 1985.
Morris, Leon. *Glory in the Cross*. London: Hodder and Stoughton, 1966.
Myers, J. D. *Nothing But the Blood of Jesus: How the Sacrifice of Jesus Saves the World from Sin*. Dallas, OR: Redeeming, 2017.
A New Catechism: Catholic Faith for Adults. New York: Herder and Herder, 1967.
O'Mahony, Gerald. *Abba! Father! A Personal Catechism*. New York: Crossroad, 1982.
Oden, Thomas C. *Classic Christianity: A Systematic Theology*. New York: HarperOne, 1992.
Olson, Roger E. "An Example of Unwarranted Theological Speculation: Divine Timelessness." https://www.patheos.com/blogs/jesuscreed/2015/02/23/is-god-timeless/.
———. *Finding God in the Shack: Seeking Truth in a Story of Evil and Redemption*. Downers Grove, IL: InterVarsity, 2009.
Origen. *On First Principles III*, vi, I. Translated by G. W. Butterworth. London: SPCK, 1936.
Packer, J. I. *Knowing God*. Downers Grove, IL: InterVarsity, 1973.
Payton, James R., Jr. *Getting the Reformation Wrong: Correcting Some Misunderstandings*. Downers Grove, IL: InterVarsity, 2010.
———. *Light from the Christian East: An Introduction to the Orthodox Tradition*. Downers Grove, IL: InterVarsity, 2007.
Peckham, John C. *The Love of God: A Canonical Model*. Downers Grove, IL: InterVarsity, 2015.
Phillips, J. B. *New Testament Christianity*. Eugene, OR: Wipf and Stock, 2012.
Phillips, John A. *Christ for Us in the Theology of Dietrich Bonhoeffer*. New York: Harper & Row, 1967.
Rahner, Karl. *Theological Investigations: Confrontations*. Theological Investigations vol. 11. Baltimore: Helicon, 1964.
Richardson, Alan, ed. *A Theological Word Book of the Bible*. New York: Macmillan, 1958.
Routledge, Robin. *Old Testament Theology: A Thematic Approach*. Downers Grove, IL: InterVarsity, 2008.
Royster, Dimitri. *The Kingdom of God: The Sermon on the Mount*. Yonkers, NY: St. Vladimir's Seminary Press, 1992.
———. *St. Paul's Epistle to the Romans: A Pastoral Commentary*. Yonkers, NY: St. Vladimir's Seminary Press, n.d.
Schmemann, Alexander. *The Celebration of Faith: Sermons*. Vol. 1. Crestwood, NY: St. Vladimir's Seminary Press, 1991.
Shaw, D. W. D. *Who Is God?* Naperville, IL: SCM Book Club, 1968.
Singer, Irving. *The Nature of Love: From Plato to Luther*. Chicago: University of Chicago Press, 1984.
Spearing, Elizabeth. *Revelations of Divine Love*. London: Penguin, 1998.

Bibliography

Stăniloae, Dumitru. *The Experience of God: Orthodox Dogmatic Theology.* Vol. 1, *Revelation and Knowledge of the Triune God.* Brookline, MA: Holy Cross Orthodox, 1994.
Swartley, Willard. *John.* Believer's Church Bible Commentary. Harrisonburg, VA: Herald, 2013.
Talbott, Thomas. *The Inescapable Love of God.* 2nd ed. Eugene, OR: Cascade, 2014.
Thiselton, Anthony C. *A Concise Encyclopedia of the Philosophy of Religion.* Grand Rapids: Baker, 2002.
———. *The Thiselton Companion to Christian Theology.* Grand Rapids: Eerdmans, 2015.
Tillich, Paul. *Systematic Theology.* 3 vols. Chicago: University of Chicago Press, 1973.
Torrance, Thomas F. *The Christian Doctrine of God, One Being Three Persons.* New York: T. & T. Clark, 2016.
Tozer, A. W. *The Knowledge of the Holy.* New York: Harper, 1961.
Underhill, Evelyn, Lumsden Barkway and Lucy Menzies, eds. *An Anthology of the Love of God: From the Writings of Evelyn Underhill.* London: A. R. Mowbray, 1953.
van den Brink, Gijsbert. *Almighty God: A Study of the Doctrine of Divine Omnipotence.* Kampen, The Netherlands: Kok Pharos, 1993.
van der Kooi, Cornelis and Gijsbert van den Brink. *Christian Dogmatics: An Introduction.* Eerdmans: Grand Rapids, 2017.
Vanhoozer, Kevin, ed. *Nothing Greater, Nothing Better.* Grand Rapids: Eerdmans, 2001.
Walsh, James, ed. *The Cloud of Unknowing.* The Classics of Western Spirituality. Mahwah, NJ: Paulist, 1981.
Ware, Bishop Kallistos. *How Are We Saved? The Understanding of Salvation in the Orthodox Tradition.* Minneapolis: Light & Life, 1996.
———. *The Orthodox Way.* Rev. ed. Crestwood, NY: St. Vladimir's Seminary Press, 1995.
Wessling, Jordan. *Love Divine: A Systematic Account of God's Love for Humanity.* New York: Oxford, 2020.
Whale, J. S. *Christian Doctrine.* London: The Religious Book Club, 1941.
White, David Manning. *Eternal Quest: The Search for God.* Vol. 1. New York: Paragon, 1991.
Wicks, Robert J. *Seeds of Sensitivity.* Notre Dame: Ave Maria, 1995.
Williams, J. P. *Seeking the God Beyond: A Beginner's Guide to Christian Apophatic Spirituality.* London: SCM, 2018.
Wilson-Hartgrove, Jonathan. "Everyone Belongs to God." *Plough Quarterly*, Summer 2015, no. 5.
Wirzba, Norman. *Way of Love: Recovering the Heart of Christianity.* New York: HarperOne, 2016.
Wright, N. T. *Broken Signposts: How Christianity Made Sense of the World.* San Francisco: HarperOne, 2012.
Zahnd, Brian. *Sinners in the Hands of a Loving God.* Colorado Springs: Waterbrook, 2017.
Zaleski, Irma. *Who Is God? The Soul's Road Home.* Boston: New Seeds, 2006.
Zizioulas, John. *Being as Communion.* Crestwood, NY: St. Vladimir's Seminary Press, 1985.

www.ingramcontent.com/pod-product-compliance
Lightning Source LLC
Chambersburg PA
CBHW031428150426
43191CB00006B/441